Decoding Our Origins
The Lived Experiences of Colombian Adoptees

Edited by Abby Forero-Hilty

Disclaimer
In the spirit of respecting the voice of the adopted person, the authors in this anthology have been given free rein to use whatever terminology they feel comfortable with when referring to themselves and their families of origin. The terms used by the individual authors do not reflect a group decision nor do they necessarily harmonize across chapters.

Book layout by Philip Harley

ISBN 978-1540833334

All proceeds from this book will go via DecodingOrigins, LLC, to provide DNA kits to Colombian adoptees and first families who are searching for their relatives.

For more information, go to www.decodingorigins.com

Please direct all correspondence to:
Abby Forero-Hilty
info@decodingorigins.com

In loving memory of
Alexander Berg and Marisa (Ana Maria) Bocanegra

Contents

Foreword

As a fellow Colombian adoptee, the invitation to write the foreword for *Decoding Our Origins: The Lived Experiences of Colombian Adoptees* is deeply humbling. I hope to convey the depth of the collection of personal stories in *Decoding Our Origins: The Lived Experiences of Colombian Adoptees*, the first published book to showcase the Colombian Adoptee Diaspora (CAD). The adoption of Colombian children grew exponentially around the world during the late 1960's through the early 2000's. Most adoption stories, particularly international adoption narratives, highlight the assumed incredible good fortune of the adopted person. Colombian adoptions, specifically, offer a broad array of storylines to confirm such narratives. Examples include poverty, drug trafficking, guerrilla warfare, and unceasing violence. However, there is another narrative that is rarely told. The collection of personal essays and poems in *Decoding Our Origins: The Lived Experiences of Colombian Adoptees* gives voice to Colombian adoptees previously unheard. Each contributor, an expert in their personal lived experience, bravely shares their journey, personal self-discovery, pain, anger, and joy. As a fellow Colombian adoptee, mother, Licensed Professional Counselor, and academic, each story felt familiar and yet, refreshingly nuanced. Adoptees of all backgrounds will find the same comfort, assurance, validation and connection within these powerful narratives.

Decoding Our Origins: The Lived Experiences of Colombian Adoptees blends standard adoption-related developmental tasks such as learning one's adoption story, longing for connection with first families and birth countries, and managing divided loyalty between adoptive and first families, with the modernity of DNA testing. International search and reunion efforts are enhanced with the power and promise of this advanced technology. Conversely, several stories highlight the reality of most CADs: little to none or false information surrounding the circumstances of their birth, relinquishment, and first families. Their voices spotlight the emerging collective awareness of the corruptive practices and circumstances related to some adoption stories as well as the oppressive situations and choices burdened by first Colombian families.

Familiar adoption themes including loss, grief, abandonment, multiple family placements, and adoption identity development are fully explored. The complexities of racial and ethnic identity development, racial isolation and discrimination, psychological trauma, and the overwhelming sense of "otherness" are honestly displayed. However, behind each story the powerful force of our inherent strengths gleaned from our Colombian ancestors, known and unknown, paired with the blossoming connections made via social media and DNA to other CADs spotlight the warrior survivor found in us all.

First family knowledge is a human right. Despite closed records, false stories, and corruptive adoption practices, adopted persons and first families are now actively utilizing DNA testing to find one another. These efforts are not without cost, however, and DNA results can create more questions than answers at times. Nonetheless, our community will continue to reclaim our first families, our heritage, and our stories. It is my profound hope that the collaborative effort of *Decoding Our Origins: The Lived Experiences of Colombian Adoptees* aid in the mission to bring together displaced and lost families via DNA testing and matching.

Dr. Susan F. Branco
Colombian Adoptee
Licensed Professional Counselor
Clinical Assistant Professor, Loyola University Maryland

Dr. Susan F. Branco is a licensed professional counselor in Virginia and Maryland. She resides in northern Virginia with her husband, daughter, and pug. She is a Nationally Certified Counselor (NCC) and an Approved Clinical Supervisor (ACS). Susan earned her BA in Human Services and MA in Rehabilitation Counseling from The George Washington University. She earned a doctorate in Counselor Education and Supervision from Virginia Tech. In addition, she holds a post-masters certificate in Marriage and Family Therapy from Virginia Tech and in Clinical Community Counseling from Johns Hopkins University. For thirteen years Susan maintained an independent clinical practice specializing in working with adults, children, and families connected to adoption and foster care. Susan's research interests examine how school and clinical mental health counselors work with transracially adopted persons and clinical supervision practices within counselor education for counselors of color. Her research is published in peer-reviewed journals and is featured in professional counseling literature.

Introduction

English is, for want of a better expression, my adoptive mother tongue. It has also become the lingua franca for much of the world. The concepts of "mother" and the mother-child relationship are so fundamental that they are deeply embedded in the English language. Examples abound and range from the charming, "Mother Nature" and "Necessity is the mother of wisdom," to the humorous, "A face only a mother could love," and the classic genre of "Yo momma" jokes (of which there are exponential variations), to the extraterrestrial sounding "mother ship," to the rude/offensive, "son of a bitch," and "motherfucker," to the superlative, "The mother of all...," and even to an old mining expression which has taken on a figurative meaning in everyday language, "the mother lode." Just to name a few.

So, what does it feel like to grow up without knowing who your mother is when you are surrounded by people and a language that take this relationship largely for granted???

For the first 36 years of my life, I did not know who my mother was. Because I had no mother who could tell me the story of my birth, I questioned if I had even been born to a real live woman. If I had never been born, then how could I possibly exist? How could I be real? Perhaps I was not...

I believe most children who grow up in adoptive families struggle with these painful questions. When I joined the Facebook group *Adopted from Colombia!* in 2009, I "met" other Colombian adoptees for the first time. I read their stories of longing to find their first mothers and families. I read how they questioned the ubiquitous idea about how adoptees had been "chosen" and should be "grateful."

I also discovered how they actively worked on regaining and incorporating their lost Colombian culture back into their lives by (re)learning Spanish, celebrating Colombian Independence Day, and enjoying Colombian music and food.

From the moment I joined, the words of these very real people with very real stories resonated with me. In turn, I came to understand that I, too, was real—always had been and always would be—whether I ever found my mother or not.

All the authors here were adopted from Colombia into non-Spanish-speaking families and countries in the USA and Europe. While they share the same start in life, they have walked different paths and processed their feelings, thoughts, and experiences differently.

There are, however, common threads that run through each of the chapters: the consequences of not knowing one's own mother and the truths about one's origins, and the unwavering pull (of DNA?) that drives the adoptee to seek out her or his roots. These commonalties question the popular notion of adoption as a "win-win-win" event. They paint a broad picture of the lifelong effects of adoption on the child-turned-adult.

After years of getting to know each other and building up trust within the cyber world of closed groups on Facebook, I am extremely proud and excited to be part of this project, where a cross-section of persons adopted from Colombia have shared their personal stories of loss, hope, grief, pride, sadness, anger, happiness, and, above all, perseverance and love. May their words provide insight and inspiration to all those who are navigating the complexities of adoption in general, and transracial and international adoption in particular.

Abby Forero-Hilty
Laufen
December 2016

Mother Colombia/Colombian Mother
Norina Vazquez (Marina Cardenas)

Someday I'm going to see you.
Will you see me?
I'm going to kiss your soil.
I'm mad I was absent for so long.
What could I do?
I was only a child.
Your daughter.
Take care of me.
I'm here.
We have time.
What's happened?

Norina Vazquez, born Marina Cardenas according to the relinquishment document provided by her orphanage in Colombia, grew up in the United States. Her life has been shaped in many ways by having both a birth family and an adoptive family. She was born in Medellín and adopted from Bogotá at age three. Norina began her search for her birth family as a teenager and is still searching for them after nearly 30 years. She considers herself bi-family and will continue her search for her other half/family until reunited. Through DNA, she has found many cousins. Norina has visited and volunteered in her Colombian orphanage, attended a Colombian university where she majored in Spanish and Latin American area studies, and worked as an international adoption coordinator. She earned her teaching degree at Cal State, Bakersfield, in 2004. She has also taken coursework in the MSW program. Currently, Norina works in a Spanish immersion school where she teaches mainly non-Spanish speaking children all of their subjects in Spanish. Norina is married and is a CASA/Guardian Ad Litem for local foster children. However, her most crucial role is that of mother to her two sons.

¿Eres Tú Mi Madre?
Carlotta Mendes (Ivette Rodriguez)

Are you my mother?, by PD Eastman, was my favorite book when I was little. It was about a baby bird that is separated from its mother and goes around asking different animals and even inanimate objects, "Are you my mother?" The baby bird almost seems desperate but that book has a happy ending. I am still waiting for mine. I don't know if it was because at the time I knew I was adopted as I honestly cannot remember, but it is and has been a very telling book for my entire adulthood as I started "the search" at 18 years old, and now find myself at the age of 43 about to turn 44 years old. Since I have been searching that long some details and times have become fuzzy, but I do want to share the bulk of my story in hopes that you might find strength and *esperanza* (hope) to not give up, to never give up looking for something that is rightfully yours.

My journey, the story I share with you, began in 1990, if not before, with questions in my mind, and it will eventually lead us to the present with the technological advancement of computers and science. I would like to share with you somewhat briefly how it started, where I am today, and why I continue with *esperanza.* I can't say I did very much to search when I was at the beginning of my journey as there were not many resources. My search was more or less just trying to find out the truth surrounding my adoption—and that itself was a difficult task. When I was younger I would ask my mother about what happened to me. This question fell on my mother alone because my parents separated and soon divorced before I was five years old. I would seem to get different stories such as, "Your parents died and your grandparents raised you until they could not anymore." But when I was 18, with determination, I demanded the truth from my mother, which made her uncomfortable and squirm as usual. "Adoption" was a subject that we "did not discuss." As I was "chosen" and a "gift," it did not matter what happened before; what mattered was that if it had not been for my mother choosing me, picking me, I probably would not even be alive. Hence, speaking and bringing up anything related to my adoption was very difficult and something done maybe once every few years if not less. This made it/me (because this was an integral part of who I was) feel like a dirty secret (but nobody picked up on that perception, honestly not even me; it wasn't until I was a full-fledged adult, maybe already in my 30s, that I would be able to put the feelings into words).

So, when I approached my mother when I was 18, she said that she did not want to tell me the truth because it would hurt me. But of course I insisted that she tell me the truth; in my mind I wondered how I could search without having the real story, as I would never be able to find my mother. She then proceeded to tell me that my mother abandoned me at the house of a man that she worked for, I think. Heck it's been so long and there have been so many stories I can't keep them straight. I also don't recall if she ever gave me my true name, but I did see it on documents.
I can say that she NEVER gave me anything to help my search, although she did say that she would help and wanted to help if she could. She would even tell me that if I wanted to go to Colombia she would pay. As the years have advanced, she has grown firm in her conviction, telling me that I will NEVER find anyone, and maintains THAT story UP TO today.

You may ask where my father fits in to all of this? My father, a wonderful man, had his challenges as I was growing up. He wrestled with the disease of alcoholism and although I did see him almost every weekend, our encounters were not very conducive to growing a relationship until I was about 19. We then became extremely close but still never spoke of anything uncomfortable; we did not even talk about death when he was in the final stages of dying from cancer when I was in my 30s. My father had a way of letting you know he was uncomfortable with a conversation by simply changing the subject, and if you didn't change it, he did until you got that he did not want to discuss the current subject. Sometimes it was subtle and other times as subtle as a jackhammer. I am very fortunate to have had an amazing relationship with him but can't say the same for my mother, as I believe how she handled the subject of my adoption created a deep resentment. Though this was not our only issue, it is quite possibly the deep underlying root of my negative feelings towards her.

So with this minimal information began what I called the "search." Keep in mind this was in 1990, so home computers weren't really big on the scene yet. I had also just had a child myself, which sparked my curiosity even more—how could it not as I looked at my child who looked like me! (Did I look like my mother?) There was also the realization with the birth of my daughter that this is the only person in this entire world that is blood related to me. There were no real ways to search and I had no resources, so the idea of a "search" was fleeting.

In 1992 I got back on the horse and decided that maybe hiring a private investigator for my search would be the answer because I had heard this to be a way of finding someone. But at that time my husband and I barely had a pot to piss in, as the saying goes when you grow up in NYC. I was just 20 and my husband 24; our daughter was only 2 years old and we could barely make the rent. So nothing ever came of it.

Around rolled 1997 and with it came the affordability of computers; they were at that point in most homes and we had one. I found adoptee chats and that sparked the search again, but it never really yielded any information other than putting me in touch and chatting with other Colombian adoptees, some even from the same orphanage that I am from, FANA. We would compare notes and we learned that many stories and paperwork were bad, illegitimate, illegal. This was not new to me, however, as my mother had revealed that she had had to pay off some people in order to get my paperwork expedited. The story there, in short, is that she went to FANA to adopt only my brother (not genetically related to me) and saw me. I was supposed to go to Holland (many adoptees from FANA were sent there), but she also then wanted me too, so in order for her to adopt me as well they had to get my paperwork together fast. That's where the illegal paperwork came in.

Around 2003, in my yearning for search and support, I came across an actual support group that met up not far from me. Those in the group highly recommended that I read the book written by the man who ran the group, and so I did. When I read *Adoption Healing...A Path to Recovery*, by Joe Soll, I literally cried, on and off, for almost three months. I couldn't explain it; I still can't other than to say it touched something so deep in my soul, so deep in my subconscious: It spoke to the child in me. It took some time but I did go to another meeting.

I went with my daughter, who was then about 13, for support, and it was an amazing experience but it made me realize how I had never taken the time to heal or even realized that I needed to heal from what is a huge traumatic event. I will be honest, since then I haven't continued to address the trauma because of how much it made me cry, and what made it worse was that I could not explain it, other than to say a gate was opened and I am better off with that gate closed.

Again no real gains. My life got really busy and I got frustrated and stopped looking as I had done before. Fast-forward to 2008; my father died, which was absolutely devastating. I went along with the grieving process for some time. Before he passed I was so close to him. He had become my support, my mother and father, my confidant, and he actually moved in with my family and me less than a year before he died, not knowing he had cancer. Though we were very close he did not like to talk about certain things, as stated earlier, and I did not dare do or say anything that would hurt him, so I never talked about my adoption with or around him. I did not do anything in terms of the searching process while he was alive, out of a deep respect, though I did still wonder and want to look. So that is why I waited until he passed to start my search once again. It was at that time that I decided to file for what is called a G639 form: The Freedom of Information Act Request Form. I had learned about this form many years earlier from the adoptee chat groups but never acted on it; however, I then felt it was time as I was getting worried because I had just lost a parent and feared that I could lose my birth parent(s) without ever meeting her/him. So I filed this form and it took quite some time; as a matter of fact, when the packet finally came in the mail, I had forgotten all about it. It was quite a thick packet that had all the papers filed through the then Department of Immigration and Naturalization (now known as Department of Homeland Security) related to my adoption. About six pages were significant but written in Spanish.

I felt like I finally had my story. I also had my birthmother's name but I was mad because this meant my mother had had my birthmother's name and had never revealed it to me. Since, at that point, and quite honestly for years before, I was not able to get anywhere with my mother as far as information, I had long given up and shut the whole adoption thing off as far as she was concerned.

I felt as though there was no point, not to mention the fact that since my father's death our relationship had deteriorated so badly that anytime we got together we ending up in a horrible yelling match.

In the beginning of 2015, one of my goals was to truly do all that was in my power to find my family. Life had carried on; so many obstacles once in my way were falling away. My focus was not quite so sharp as before on my children because at the time they were 24 and 18 (my turn to focus on me), my career was stable as I no longer had to work at growing it, having been a nurse for eight years at that point, and the finances were just not as tough as once upon a time. It was time to do a DNA test. This was and is the "yellow brick road" to finding people. It was a huge step for me.

In February of 2015, the test results were an eye opener, as I did not expect to find out the mix of ancestries that I was. And I was pleased that there was one truth that my adoptive mother had told me, which was that I was indigenous, though not pure, but I did have Native American blood and a small portion was Amazonian. Though the results did not put me in contact with anybody closely related, which of course would have been ideal, I am happy to know what I am for sure. The particular company I chose to do my DNA test with was not very big in Colombia; had I known that I would not have gone forward with that company. But as with all things, DNA testing is a learning process, so after some time I learned that another company (Family Tree DNA [FTDNA]) was a bit more popular in Colombia, meaning more people there use that test, and so I paid to test with them. I have also uploaded my results with other companies that have large databanks that many other people upload their results to as well. I just hope and pray that the right person will upload their DNA to the same databank or companies I have used.

With the DNA test results, the next step was to hire a search organization and, within a few weeks, in March I believe, somebody contacted me. I initially thought this woman was with the search company but later found out the she had come across my information, started asking me questions about my search, and about 15 minutes into the conversation, which I had to translate via Google Translate, she told me that she thought she knew who my mother is! I was in disbelief; she told me the name and then showed me the picture. I was sitting in bed with my husband, who couldn't believe the resemblance. While this was happening I was also messaging my daughter and sent her the picture; she agreed with my husband. My daughter, being tech savvy, put a picture of this woman and me together in a collage and my husband was floored. What was I to say or do? I asked if she could do a DNA test, as I did not want to believe until it was confirmed, because that is the gold standard nowadays.

The woman that was a suspected match did not have a lot of money by American standards. She had already taken a DNA test once to try and match with a person in another country, but they did not match and they had not used FTDNA. Only a few weeks prior, I had read about a GoFundMe to help those that cannot afford the $100 US dollar fee to get a DNA test done. I wanted her to do the FTDNA test, that way, if she was not a match for me, she still had a good chance of possibly finding her daughter through FTDNA. I got in touch with the founder of the GoFundMe project and there was a kit available in Bogotá, I just had to put in some money. The problem was that this woman lived 12 hours away by car from Bogotá. At first we waited to see how she could get there, knowing she lacks the funds most Americans have, and after some time and conversing with her son we figured out that she has a brother that lives in Bogotá. So rather than put the financial stress on her or her sons we moved forward and decided to do the DNA test on her brother, who was happy to help. He went to get his cheeks swabbed and then did the waiting game as it took some time and worry over how to get the test to the US in a timely fashion and with what carrier due to customs and the question as to whether or not it was a medical biohazard.

During the time that it took to wait for the shipping and results of the test, I often, almost on a daily basis, spoke with the woman's son— who could have potentially been my half-brother. It was amazing to have this relationship with a sibling that I had never had. He was so incredibly sweet, patient, and caring. Once in a while I would allow my mind to think how nice it would be if he was truly my blood brother, but then I would have to pull my mind and heart away because if he was not, if she was not, it was going to be very painful. This was something I wanted so bad, something I have wanted all my life.

This family is big and accepting and they wanted to know about me; I was trying to keep some distance but they made it hard. Finally, one day, he asked me what I would tell his mother if I found out that she was not my mother. In my mind I have to be honest because he was only looking out for his mother's interest, but I was not ready to open that emotional door. However, I felt I had to because if the tables were turned I would want to know the same thing, and I answered him as best I could using Google translate, knowing that some of this was going to get lost in translation. He deserved an honest answer for wanting to protect her; she had been through this once before and I can't imagine the pain of having to go through the process of hope all over again. That was it for me for the next two days; I was emotionally spent. I could not talk to him and even though he tried to get me to talk he could not understand my feelings. How could he? How could anyone?

The conversation left me pondering whether or not I was prepared for the outcome. I questioned myself, *I think I am prepared for either result!?!* That is a huge statement; if the result was that we were not family, then I had gotten closer and taken the biggest step toward finding my mother than I ever had in the past—and that speaks volumes. If the results were positive, I now had this big family that I quickly learned has some dynamics of their own, but I would prepare to go to Colombia and meet the family I had dreamed of my whole life. With this family I would not have to worry about rejection as some adoptees have faced.

So, on June 29, 2016, I opened the app on my phone to find the results were in. I was afraid to look at the results by myself so I woke my husband up and then we looked together...MY HEART SANK RIGHT INTO MY STOMACH. IT WAS NOT WHAT I WAS HOPING FOR. THERE WAS NO CONNECTION! My name was nowhere on the relations list indicating a blood connection or relation! I tried to hold it together while my husband asked what it said. I mustered up the strength to tell him, "We are not related." I tried to keep the tears inside. I was not supposed to have emotionally invested my heart but it had built up without me realizing, under the surface, like an iceberg. I was hurt; honestly, I was devastated. I fought back tears, on and off, for about a week, never allowing myself to fully lose it, because I needed to be and feel strong and in control. I was also afraid that if I started crying and fully feeling what was inside I would never stop crying. I did not want to feel like a lost child or should I dare say like the lost child I have always felt I am. I cried mostly when alone, not letting anyone in my family know how deep this cut. I could never let them see me as weak; they need to know that I am strong for them.

My next task was to tell this guy, who would have made an amazing brother, and whom I had been talking to since March, but I couldn't tell him that day because I had to cope with my own feelings. I also had to let my kids know because this affected them as well, as my daughter had told me during the process. I had not realized that they were affected because they are grown now, but, as my daughter said, this was potentially finding their family too! And that had made both of my kids excited, so when I did tell them they were supportive of my feelings but were disappointed at the loss of potential family as well. It took me a few days, a week to be honest, to muster up the courage to tell the man who I thought was my half-brother. At first he was sad, but then hit me with the notion that his uncle (the woman's brother that actually took the DNA test) may not be a blood relation! What? Is this really happening.... Is this a *telenovela*??? If he is not a blood relation to the woman I suspect may be my mother, than this test was basically for nothing. I asked him for details but he was unable to tell me; he said that he needed to talk to his uncle for the details. To make a long story short, after a few weeks, he told me that the uncle was in fact the blood brother of his mother (the woman I thought months earlier may possibly be my mother). And once again the tears rolled down.

At the beginning of this DNA matching process I had pushed with this family to go through FTDNA to test, as stated earlier, so that if we did not match this woman looking for her daughter could be in the database (even though it is her brother whose DNA is on file, it would still help her). But being that we didn't match I feel as though I now have two burdens—one to find my mother and the other to find a woman's daughter.

There were two things I felt from the beginning of this process that I had only mentioned to my daughter and maybe my husband: #1 I did not feel this was "it," but my husband and daughter thought that "feeling" was my deep inner self being protective, and #2 that I was meant to help find this woman's daughter if she was not my mother.
With that being said, I have their DNA info and so as long as God gives me strength to look for my own mother I will look for her daughter; every time I log on to check my own DNA matching I check her family's data as well.

Upon finding out that we were not a match, a friend asked me what I was going to do from here: Give up? NO! I did not come this far to give up, so I will brush myself off and look again. I am not going to lie; when I look on Facebook and see so many people searching it is discouraging. There are brief moments I cry to my husband, but I cannot give up.
I have been told lies all my life and my mother admits that my paperwork is untrue. That is not unique to my case—many Colombian adoptees don't have their real names and their paperwork is filled with lies. But I encourage ALL Colombian adoptees to get their DNA tested and to use FTDNA (as well as other companies, if desired), because they seem to be the only company that is used in Colombia.

It is us that benefit. Our paperwork may be full of lies, our adoptive parents may have filled our ears with lies, and granted that's not true for all of us, but our DNA is not a lie. Our DNA is the TRUTH of who we are.

It will speak of where we come from; it will reveal our names, eventually. So those of you who don't have birthdates, names, *cédula* numbers, or the name of your mother, remember you have your DNA and nobody can take that from you—so you have the last laugh. USE it and find your truth.

Carlotta Mendes (Ivette Rodriguez) is the mother of two grown children: a 26-year-old daughter who is finishing a degree in psychology and engaged to be married in late 2017, and a 20-year-old son who is studying to be a sports writer and currently working for an AA advanced baseball team in Tampa, Florida. Carlotta has been married for 26 years to the love of her life, an amazing father, husband, and provider. Her family has been incredibly supportive every step of the way as she has walked this journey of adoption and searching. They ride the roller coaster side by side with her and long for her dreams to come true.

Once Upon A Time
Marianne Dupuis

Children love stories. They love telling and being told stories.

"Once upon a time"... But we cannot start a story from nothing, can we? Our identity is shaped throughout intimate stories (parents, families, relatives) and cultural stories (influenced by our country, by our cultural environment, by our language, by society).

How are we supposed to tell our own story when our roots are missing? When there is a blank of several months, several years?

When I was asked to write about adoption, I immediately said yes. What an amazing project to offer DNA kits to mothers trying to find their children and adoptees trying to find their mothers/families.

But then I hesitated for some time because I did not know where to start: I never talk about my adoption in front of my family. Not talking about it has been a reality for many years. I never felt I had the authorisation to talk about it. I never got any "space for talking." Adoption was considered "a minor event from the past," and I was a little girl, who never asked for anything, conforming to (and coping with) that reality. I put all my questions and emotions aside for many years. When I was 34, I started to dare to dream about researching my adoption. My adoption was done in secrecy; all traces seem to have been erased. No one talked about it, so neither did I.

I do not like talking about my story because, truth be told, I don't know anything other than what I was told.

My adoption is not official. I have no official documents.

My adoptive parents and a couple of friends lived and worked in Tumaco. One day, the Archbishop of Tumaco, Archbishop Irizar Salazar, asked them if they were willing to adopt a child. The same day, another Belgian couple (my parents' friends) also adopted a little girl in Medellín.

My parents came to get me at the Luz Castro Clinic in Medellín. I think I was two and a half months old. In Tumaco, a doctor made a false birth certificate under my adoptive mother's name. The Archbishop then baptized me. That was it. After that, the Belgian Embassy (in Colombia) declared me as being a Belgian child born in Colombia.

On my ID papers, I am Belgian; I was born in Tumaco although I was born in Medellín.

"Who are you?
Where are you today?
Do I have brothers, sisters?
Why did you abandon me?
Did you wish to keep me?"

I am 52 years old and I still don't have any answers.

The adoption gave me parents. They loved me; they supported me while I was growing up.

My adoptive parents told me about my adoption.

A paediatrician advised them to talk to me about it as soon as possible so that I would consider it a positive thing. An act of love from a woman who wanted a better and happier life for her child!

This is a beautiful theory, but a theory eluding the most important point: I really experienced and felt that I was abandoned and then entrusted to strangers. As a result, I feel a great deal of anger. I have a feeling of "oddness." A feeling of alienation, of not being in the right place at the right moment. When I think about it I realise that I have always been there for my relatives, my friends, and my children, but have never really been available for myself. This is a point I am working on today: self-availability. The second point is that I feel something has been taken away from me. My identity was taken away; by refusing to officialise my adoption, my roots were cut.

I shared someone's life for nine months.

"I shared everything; I felt everything.
Your joys, your pains, your fears...
I shared it all."

"Silence settled between us.
Did you think this silence would be good for me?"

I lost my mother but I believe I am still connected to her genetically, psychologically.

Perhaps spiritually.

During the nine months we shared, I experienced what I think is a constitutive experience, the conscious and unconscious base that has deeply impacted on my spiritual experience. I believe that this is at the heart of the life I was given and the life I received; upon this my foundations were built. And I believe I came to this world with pre-existing tendencies in terms of personality and behaviour. For example, I was raised by non-religious parents and I cannot explain why I have always been so attracted to religion, faith, and churches since I was a little girl. When I was six years old, I wished I could become a sister (in the religious sense). When I think about the woman who gave birth to me, I see a woman who could not speak for herself; I feel her helplessness. I bear the unconscious burden of my ancestors. I bear a past legacy. I have it inside of me but I am not familiar with it. To know who I am I have to know where I come from.

I keep on hoping, waiting, looking.

Today, thanks to Facebook, a great number of us are able to communicate, to share. One dares to talk about adoption. One dares to look for one's biological family. One dares to look for one's child put up for adoption.

Today, I am very happy to be in touch with other Colombian adoptees via Facebook. It allows me to share but also to reflect on my own difficulties. When an adoptee explains he has difficulties to communicate, when an adoptee talks about his difficulties, it echoes in me and reminds me of my own difficulties.
But it also allows me to put words to certain feelings I had put aside. When I see an adoptee finally achieving his goal of finding his natural family, I feel a lot of joy.

Am I actively searching? I started my search about 20 years ago but I have not been constant in the process. Sometimes I (re)search compulsively, meaning intensively for months, and whenever I feel disappointed I stop searching for periods of variable length. However, the strength of our Facebook group, *Adopted from Colombia!* (for Colombian adoptees and their families) and its support make me say that I will never stop looking.

Marianne was adopted in 1964 from Medellín when she was two or three months old. She grew up and worked in Africa. Marianne has four children — three biological children and one child adopted in 1997 from Cali, Colombia. She has been living in Belgium since 1997. Marianne is divorced. She works for social services with families and children up to 18 years of age. She loves her family, reading, traveling, and human contact. Her biggest dream is to meet someone from her biological family.

Abandoned By Two Mothers

Diana Zea Martinez

A few years ago, I never thought I would be writing a piece like this on such a bittersweet topic. I never knew how powerful the word "mother" would become to me in so many different ways.

Initially, especially in childhood and even early adulthood, if someone had asked me about what the word "mother" meant to me, I would have gladly and proudly talked about my adoptive mother. We were always so close. I have so many happy memories of shopping with her, sitting next to her by our pool, watching her cook, watching television soap operas with her, and her rocking me in a special rocking chair whenever I was sad or hurting. We seemed to be so alike, or so she told me. My grandmother (her mother) would tell me how I could not possibly be adopted because our brains were identical (smart, opinionated, driven, and tender hearted). I would eventually tell people how I was obviously meant to be her daughter and she was meant to be my mother because of how "connected" we were. She would brag about my accomplishments as a kid and young adult. It used to make me uncomfortable; especially when she would tell random strangers how "wonderful" I was even though she didn't "create" me. If only I had a nickel for every time she just had to tell someone I was adopted from Colombia. I clearly became her "golden child." I was very torn as a child when my mom would explain that I was adopted from another country. On one hand I was relieved as it brought an end to the stares. On the other, I was embarrassed. I was embarrassed because it underscored my differences and placed me into a category that had negative connotations. Surely people would think I was the product of the drug war in Colombia and/or praise my adoptive mother for "saving me."

Milestones

As a female adoptee, I inevitably reached one of those milestone moments in a girl's life that should be handled very delicately, especially if you're adopted...starting my period. It seems that daughters may enter this milestone in life around the same time as their birthmothers as it could be some sort of reference point.

However, in my case, I had no way of knowing when my birthmother started her period. There was something awkward and strange to me in talking about my body and development with my non-biologically-related mother. I cannot really explain why but it just seemed weird knowing my body parts would be nothing like hers. I will never forget the day when I was 14 years old and that moment came, being one of the last of my friends to cross this threshold into young womanhood. But rather than having an experience like most of my friends did, where their mothers whisked them away to a "celebratory" lunch and to purchase their feminine products together, I had a horrible experience. Instead, my adoptive mother had my dad (with my little brother in tow) drop me off at a pharmacy and I had to buy the stuff by myself.

It was such a humiliating and embarrassing moment in my life. Inside I felt like it wasn't right, but who was I to question it? So it just made that already awkward moment in life even more awkward for me.

Another milestone came when I went away to college, and my adoptive mother and I had an argument in the car. The outcome was that she drove me straight to the drop-off area for new students, reached over, opened my passenger-side door, and kicked me out. She literally said, "Get out!" and left me standing there. Part of the reason this was so traumatic for me is that I literally felt abandoned. My adoptive mother physically kicked me out of the car at a time when I needed her comfort and support. I was going away to college and she left me. And it was exacerbated when I had to confront my roommate whose mother was there, acting as a mother should. I felt so alone, in a new environment, around new people. Perhaps subconsciously it bothered me, as it was a reminder of being "abandoned" as a baby and being taken to a new place surrounded by new people.

Along the way, there were a couple of boyfriends and life decisions I made that she didn't agree with and her way of handling it was to just ignore me and give me the silent treatment...not for hours, not for days, but for months at a time. Again, these were times where I needed a mother but instead I felt rejected and abandoned by her. On top of that, I was confused and was left feeling anxious. I was anxious about what I did wrong to upset her. I eventually learned it was not about me. But that took years.

Unfortunately, I have never met nor do I have enough information to find my birthmother. Growing up, my adoptive mother talked about her as if she were some angel who loved me so much she wanted a better life for me that she couldn't give me. I could not really wrap my head around that notion. How could someone love you so much that they could leave you? It didn't feel like love to me. It was the same old song and dance many adoptees get without the facts to substantiate it. I have since learned that my paperwork is inaccurate and my adoption likely part of a very corrupt system, leading me to believe I was illegally trafficked rather than legitimately abandoned or relinquished. In fact, despite my adoptive mother encouraging me my entire life to search for my birthmother, she not only refused to help me (the way I needed her to help me), she completely sabotaged me and stood up for the corrupt orphanage I came from and defended them rather than helping me and empathizing with my situation.

My whole life I had this image of my birthmother as young and full of love for me despite giving me up, even though at times I didn't understand it. I was taught and influenced to think this was all a wonderful thing, and I was never made aware of the trauma that actually occurred. I learned of this trauma while reading the book *The Primal Wound: Understanding the Adopted Child* by Nancy Newton Verrier. As an adult, I started realizing the story of my birth and relinquishment did not make sense. How could my birthmother be too poor to take care of me yet come from a prominent wealthy family? How could she feel she could not give me a good life yet be studying to be a concert pianist while my birth father was in engineering school? Too many unanswered questions and too many lies is what it came down to. Lies that came directly from the orphanage and passed on to many adoptive parents. Stories told to kids that would mold their definitions of "mother." Nothing good can come of lies, even if the best intent is there. I think that adoption should not be so sugar coated and romanticized. Adoptive parents should be made aware of the impacts of separation of mother and child so that they can emotionally prepare their children and navigate their lives with that lens on, not the rose colored ones they are given along with their baby and adoption paperwork. It does not matter what background the family of origin had, a baby has been separated from all he or she has known and that is ALL that matters. The biological need to be with the woman who carried you for nine months has been disrupted and the impact is so great and will (not may) impact who they become as adults.

The Gift of Motherhood

Growing up, I always knew I wanted a child of my own, when the time was right. When that day finally came, it changed me forever. Everything I ever thought I knew about being a mother and about my mothers changed. It was an epiphany and saying it was a life changing moment is an understatement. In my experience, there is just something so special to me as an adoptee (especially one who was in a closed adoption process) with regards to having a child. From the day I learned I was pregnant and throughout my pregnancy, I thought about my birthmother more than I ever had before. I realized she was my mother in a way I had never thought of before. She was responsible for me during all of those months. She felt me move and kick. Perhaps she sang to me. Perhaps she really wanted me. I may never know. But for the first time, I saw her as more than this angel who loved me so much she had to give me away. I realized how she must have bonded with me. I started wondering about and questioning everything I thought I knew about her.

Then on the day I gave birth, I inevitably thought about her and what she went through during labor. How painful in more ways than one it must have been for her. Knowing that her time of "caring" for me was coming to an end. According to the staff at my orphanage, I was born at my orphanage through a special program for pregnant mothers. I am assuming she probably didn't get an epidural. So, I, in turn, decided to turn down the drugs so that I could feel what she went through to give me life (though I eventually had to get the epidural and had a cesarean section). When I first saw my daughter and touched her and held her, my life as I knew it was over. I finally felt a love that I had never experienced before. Not for anyone. She was mine and I was hers. We were each other's. She needed me. I needed her. She filled a huge hole in my heart. A hole I didn't realize needed to be filled. But in those first few days, hormone-fueled thoughts kept creeping in. All of a sudden I asked myself, "How could she have given me up?" I didn't understand and I cried big alligator tears about it. How could a mother give up her child, no matter the situation?

I flip-flopped between anger and shock that a person could do such a thing. I had fleeting moments of anger, wondering if she didn't love me, knowing the love I felt for my daughter was so unbelievably strong that I would never let her go. I questioned not only her love for me but also how someone could possibly take me away from my birthmother and send me across the world. I may never reconcile those mixed feelings unless I find her and ask her what happened. In the meantime, I may always bounce between wondering how she could give me up and how someone could take me away from her. The many feelings and emotions I felt were almost overwhelming. It caused me to hug and cuddle and love my newborn daughter even more and to tell her that I would never let her go.

After giving birth and in the weeks following, my adoptive mother was not there for me emotionally or physically in the manner in which I had always dreamed. I had pictured her side by side with me, helping me and teaching me about being a mother to a newborn. The reality was far from my dream. That was such a loss for me. I realized my loss was for not only the birthmother I did not have but also the adoptive mother I clearly wished I had. I also realized there were so many blanks that could not be filled in. I probably felt a need to re-enact a bond I thought my adoptive mother had with me and replace one that I never had a chance to develop with my birthmother. I felt so alone and helpless with this beautiful baby dependent upon me to give her everything she needed both physically and emotionally. In a sense, I did not even know where to start because I realized I was never provided any of these things fully from either of my mothers. I was left with just reading books, but mostly I trusted my gut.

Several months after our daughter was born, I was on the phone with my adoptive mother and we had a falling out. It wasn't the first, as I mentioned before, but this time was different because I was not going to go groveling back to her, desperate for her approval and acceptance. This time I was done. This time she hit me way below the belt. Not only did she tell me she wished she weren't my adoptive mother, she also gave away the special rocking chair that she used to rock me in as a child that she promised she would pass on to me. She gave it away to a distant relative who was in the blood lineage, and she did so out of spite. She did not directly give blood relation as a reason; however, after reading her "heartfelt" justifications for presenting it to a blood relative instead of me, who was adopted and not related to the original owner of the gift, I would not qualify given her new criterion. This hurt so much. The rocking chair was one of the only things that I actually associated with good memories of my adoptive mother. I held onto those memories and looked forward to sharing those memories with my daughter as well. But she took that away from me. She took it all away from me, the memories, the sentimental value, and the love that it represented. This coupled with being told she was sorry she was my adoptive mother, I am not sure I have ever been so hurt in my entire life.

So, I picked myself up and made two important decisions. First, I decided to turn the situation into a what-I-would-not-do-as-a-mother lesson. I decided that it was my mission in life to never make my daughter feel the way I felt or make her question her love for me. Second, I chose to get off of my adoptive mother's emotional roller coaster, in which she was in the driver's seat, because I was tired of riding on it my whole life and I certainly was not going to take my family for a ride on that emotional death trap. I was done. On many levels it was freeing to get off her emotional roller coaster. For the first time in my life, I did not have to worry about what my adoptive mother was going to say or do to hurt me. But at the same time, I am left with this overwhelming feeling of abandonment. All I can think about is, "Who will be my mom now? What mother figure will I share my experiences as a mother with?" These are the things I was supposed to be able to share with my mom. It makes me incredibly sad that she is missing so much and has no relationship with her "granddaughter." Even when I told her how much it hurt me that she would do and say those hurtful things to me and that I would never say that I wished she were not my mother, she never apologized. She never took accountability. She never expressed empathy.

I suppose I had many opportunities in the past to get off the roller coaster. But I don't think I had realized the ride I was on. I did not realize or accept that my adoptive mother is an emotionally ill person and has been from the day I was put in her arms at the orphanage. It wasn't until I became a mother myself that I realized the impact trauma in your own life can have on your ability to be a good parent. As a result, I am thankful for the many hours of time I have spent at critical times in my life in a therapist's office to address abandonment and separation issues. Everyone has issues from time to time, and I am glad I took the time and did the work necessary to try and resolve mine. It should be a prerequisite to parenting.

After the rocking chair incident, it was with the help of a therapist and reading several articles and books that I realized that my adoptive mother suffers from mental illness. I grew to learn about how her traumas impacted me and I live to tell about being raised by a mother who chose to never resolve those traumas. Having read up on what she likely suffers from, I again felt a sense of closure and freedom after years of trauma and endless roller coaster rides with her. I then began to feel some empathy for her. It all made sense and I began to feel sadness for her. Sadness that her trauma and her illness overpowered her life so much that she has chosen to not have a relationship with her only daughter and only granddaughter. I took this information and it gave me even more determination to raise our daughter under the principles of attachment parenting and to do everything in our power to not cause trauma for our daughter—to not set her up for these sorts of challenges in her life. Although my daughter is still a toddler, I make sure she knows she is loved. I show her and I tell her. I listen to her and I help her identify her feelings. I want her to know she is heard and she is loved. I know I am not the perfect parent. No one is. However, it is my mission in life to raise an emotionally healthy human being.
This is it. She is my one and only. She is and may be the only flesh and blood I ever know. This is my one shot. I don't get another chance. I love being a mother and honestly feel I was born to be a mother.

Perhaps my experience as both an adoptee and a daughter of a mentally unhealthy mother will make me that much better of a mother.

In my opinion, the mother-child relationship is our first relationship. It sets the tone for the rest of our relationships for the rest of our lives. It sets the tone for how we determine who we trust. It shapes our confidence and self-esteem. It models how we define love. It really is the most critical relationship from the moment we take our first breath. And quite honestly, the bond starts in utero and there is a lot of research out there to support this notion. As an adoptee, the critical, healthy mother-daughter bond literally was taken away from me in more ways than one. So as a mother, I take my role very seriously. Because for me, it is a matter of life and death.

I am so committed to being the best mom I can be that I decided to put my high-powered career on hold for a few years to devote all my time to her. We even moved across the country to a small town to make it happen. It was the best decision I ever made. She is our one and only child and I can literally throw myself into being a mother and focus on being the mother I never had. Honestly, part of the reason I felt such a magnetic pull to stay home with her during her early years is because she is my only blood relative that I know of at this time. I felt I just could not miss out on one moment with her. The bond I have developed with her is amazing and incredibly strong.

Raising her helps me get through and forget about the pain of being motherless. I thank God every day for this gift of motherhood. I will never take it for granted. I will cherish every moment. I am a survivor and a fighter. And I will be here for my daughter. Love must come first in this family.

Diana Zea Martinez was adopted at only ten days old. She was raised in the deep south of the US and went to college (on an athletic scholarship) and graduate school in the Midwest, obtaining both a BA in Psychology and an MA in Counseling. After spending several years in the Midwest, she lived many years on the west coast before again relocating with her husband to the Midwest to focus on raising their daughter. Prior to putting her career on hold, she held a high-level management position at a large organization. Diana enjoys traveling, hiking, backpacking, mountain biking, trail running, and dancing. Although she has not been reunited with her biological family, she has been back to Colombia twice and looks forward to taking her daughter there some day. She has not given up on her search for biological family and will continue to pray for justice and resolution in her and other fellow adoptees' cases.

Lost And Found
Alexis Maria McCambry

Orphan, abandoned, motherless, vulnerable, disadvantaged, neglected. So many words that could describe one child, a young infant girl who was found in a godforsaken environment with people who were involved in criminal activity during the hot summer of 1981. This young girl was lucky to be alive despite having such poor health and damage done to her body while only a baby approximately five months of age.

Colombian Authorities

It will all be okay. For we will give her what she needs in life. She will be called Ada. Her birthdate will be January 1, 1981. Now all she needs is a family to take care of her and raise her. Until we find this family to take Ada, let's place her in an orphanage.

Some time has passed and it looks as though there is a potential new family for this little girl. Let's place Ada in a foster home in the meantime while the adoption process and all of the legal documentation gets taken care of. Of course now that she is in her new foster home, let's call her Maria del Socorro Orozco. At this point the little girl is almost two and walking. She is oblivious to what is occurring around her but is very resilient. Oh! We need to send the new potential family a picture and some information about this little girl. Let's give her a new name. Her new name is Alexis Maria.

Finally the day has come when Alexis's new family has arrived all the way from the United States! This will be a great opportunity for this little girl. She has no idea how lucky she is to have been placed with these Americans who can give her a life far better than any here in Barranquilla, Colombia. This little girl will be able to grow up as a citizen of the States and live the American dream!

We want a little girl so desperately!! A daughter to call our own! Yes, we have four children of our own that we love dearly. But God has only blessed us with boys and I've been longing for a girl. Don't I deserve a daughter whom I can share girl times with such as fixing her hair and painting her nails? I'm much too old to start all over again with another baby—and what if it were another boy!!

We began our search for our daughter in 1981 and after many headaches, tears, and frustration we finally saw a light at the end of the tunnel in the spring of 1983. For, on May 16, 1983, we received the first photo of you in the mail with the name Ada Alexis printed on the back of it. I was so excited about this that I couldn't wait to call everyone with the amazing news!

We had a scare in July of 1983 when we had spoken with Beatriz (your foster mother) and were told that you were referred to as Maria and you were malnourished. I contacted Beatriz with concerns such as I was told that your name was Ada and the first picture showed a healthy little girl! Beatriz assured me that everything was all right and that you were the same little girl from the photo but that you were slightly malnourished. She also assured us that she would send more photos.

On August 11, 1983, we finally received 13 photos of you and were relieved to see that indeed you were the same girl from the original photo but slightly thinner. We were concerned about your well-being but knew that we couldn't do anything about this until we brought you safely home with us.

The day finally came on August 26, 1983, when we got on that airplane and went all the way to Colombia to get our daughter that we'd waited so many years for.

As soon as we arrived in Barranquilla, after what seemed like the longest flight ever, we located Beatriz and her son Rodrigo in the airport. We immediately asked Beatriz "How is Maria?!"

Beatriz replied with, "She's fine. Would you like to go meet her?" She didn't have to ask us that question twice! We definitely did!

As we were on our way to meet you, Rodrigo kept saying how happy you were and how you were always smiling and how much we would like you. Rodrigo was obviously very fond of you, as he had helped Beatriz take care of you before we came down there.

After what seemed like forever we finally arrived at the home of Gloria de Diaz, where you were staying. The little house was at the end of a dirt road. We almost jumped out of the car as we pulled up and were met by Gloria. I will always remember your father striding straight through the house to the back fenced yard where he first saw you, with your little head down, sitting on the back stoop with a dog. You looked so sad. You suddenly smiled as your father picked you up and continued smiling as he carried you towards me. We fed you soup and bread along with coffee spiked with milk.

On August 31, 1983, we were finally able to leave Barranquilla and head to Bogotá. Your father and Beatriz went to ICBF *(Instituto Colombiano de Bienestar Familiar*; governmental institution that handles adoptions in Colombia) one last time to get a letter and take a chance that immigration would accept it. We spent a few days in Bogotá shopping and exploring when finally the big day came. September 4, 1983, at approximately 9:00 a.m., we passed the last crucial checkpoint as we handed the immigration officer the letter from ICBF. We had our fingers crossed and held our breath as he inspected the letter. He finally waved us on after what felt like eternity.

We flew across Colombia and Barranquilla for the final trip home, and we felt a huge sense of relief as we landed in the Miami terminal and saw the "Welcome to the United States of America" sign. We were finally home with our new daughter, Alexis Maria.

It's so hot and I'm so alone. I don't know who these people are that are around me and I'm a little scared. Now all of a sudden I have to live with some new people. They tell me that I'm going to be getting a new mommy and daddy very soon and going to a place called America. I hope my new mommy and daddy like me! What is this place called America that everyone keeps talking about? Is it far away? Will I have fun there? Will there be other little kids I play with?

What if my new brothers don't like me? I have so many questions but am too scared to ask.

Today I met my new mommy and daddy. They are very different than my people I see everyday. They are white skinned and talk in a funny way. They are very kind and I'm really happy that I can finally call someone Mommy and Daddy, like normal children. They feed me soup and bread and give me lots of hugs and kisses. I don't think I've received this much affection in all my life!

Well, today is the big day! I'm so excited but scared. We got on the plane and now we are high up in the sky and I can see the water under us. The plane then started shaking and I was so frightened that I hugged tightly to my new mommy hoping to find comfort with her. Finally the plane has calmed down and I'm getting very sleepy.

The next four years, from 1983-1987, were a whirlwind of activity for the family, gradually transcending into much emotional, psychological, and occasional physical abuse.

Summer of 1987

I was six and a half years old and had just found out that I was going to have a new mom and dad yet again! I was glad about this, though, because I was very unhappy in my first adoptive family, and I could tell that my mommy didn't like me very much. I started to have doubts that this new family would keep me, so I began testing the limits. I would steal or lie and then ask afterwards, "Well are you going to give me away now?"

I loved to sing as a child and I would make up song lyrics and sing them very loudly around the house. "Will you keep me? Do you love me? Do I get to stay!?"

Growing Up as an Adoptee

As the years passed by, I had what I considered to be a fairly normal childhood from 7 to 13 years of age.
As I was becoming a teenager I started having unsettling thoughts about my past. I actually began having very vivid dreams, and my birthmother would show up in them. I fell into a deep depression to the point of suicidal thoughts and began to self-harm just to attempt to separate that emotional pain from my body.

My parents, therapists, psychologists, and school counselors didn't know how to help me, so that's how I found myself in a residential mental facility for approximately seven months. My eyes were opened to so many behaviors and lifestyles that I had been sheltered from before. I can honestly say that during that short stay I completely lost my self-identity.

My parents didn't recognize me anymore and feared for me and the situation I was in. I was moved yet again, but not back home. I was placed in a children's group home for all sorts of troubled teens. At that moment I felt that I was given up once again. I lived in that group home for the next two and a half years until I was 18 years old. I then declared that I no longer needed the meds which turned me into a zombie or that place ever again. My parents allowed me to return home in order to finish out my senior year of high school.

I got a job, began my senior year at a joint vocational high school, and started driving. It wasn't long before I began my destructive behavior yet again. This time it involved body piercing, tattoos, drugs and alcohol. I abruptly moved out of my parents' home by my actual choice this time. (Why wait for them to kick me out?)

I almost didn't graduate high school due to skipping so many days, but miraculously I did. I got pregnant around prom and that's when I made my mind up that I needed to change. I was NOT going to abandon my child; I was determined that I would be a good mother. I married my boyfriend (the baby's father) just before he left for Navy basic training.

Fast-forward 11 years later. It wasn't until just before I was supposed to leave for my job training with the Army for six months that I began to notice the huge impact my abusive marriage was having on my boys. Eleven years, two marriages (same man), three children, and many scars later, I finally had the courage to leave an abusive situation for good. I had begun to think that maybe I deserved this life, or maybe this was just my fate. I quickly wised up and between the help from a very educated therapist, a good lawyer, my own strength and courage, and God, I was able to change my mindset and grow into a healthy woman.

I became a competitive distance runner again which I hadn't done since I was 14. I started MMA (mixed martial arts) training and even successfully completed basic law enforcement training. I did all of this not only for self-defense knowledge but also to boost my self-esteem and self-confidence.

As of recently I have decided that I'm at the stage of my life where I am ready and prepared to find my birth family. I am going through the steps carefully and not rushing anything. I submitted my DNA earlier this year to FamilyTree DNA and have only discovered a few third to fifth cousins and numerous distant cousins. My next step is to forward all of my international adoption information and a page with answers to many questions about myself and why I am seeking my birth family to a contact at ICBF in Colombia.

Hopeful, resentful, chosen, empty, full of dreams. So many words that could describe the thoughts and emotions of one child who's grown up into a courageous, self-confident, scarred, and protective mother.

Alexis Maria McCambry was found when she was just an infant in Barranquilla, Colombia, in the summer of 1981. She was placed in an orphanage until she was approximately one and a half years old and then lived with a foster family until her adoption in September 1983. The first adoptive family worked with Dr. Arribe and his wife Beatriz until they were able to bring Alexis Maria to their home in Indiana, United States.

The situation with the first adoptive family did not work out due to abuse and emotional instability. Alexis Maria was therefore adopted yet again when she was six and a half years old into a family from Ohio.

Alexis Maria is now divorced with three sons and resides in eastern North Carolina. She earned her BS in Family and Consumer Science and is currently a clinical lab technician II at a prestigious hospital in Durham, North Carolina.

Dear Mother, I'm Still Here
Eric D. Johnson

My name is Eric Johnson, but lately, more than ever, you could also call me Elkin Ernesto Mosquera-Guillen. That was the name given to me in the hospital where I was born in Bogotá, Colombia, in early August of 1991. I was adopted within one week of being born, a prearranged closed adoption done by my adoptive family living outside of a town called Park Rapids, Minnesota, USA. My adoptive family moved around a bit, but finally we settled in the small town of Fergus Falls, Minnesota. Growing up in a tight-knit quiet conservative town was idyllic, every part of that picket fence Middle America aesthetic. Other parts were uncomfortable, alienating, confusing, and isolating as a small child growing into young adulthood.

I love my adoptive family dearly and grew up with the comfortable middle class privilege of a white American family, except for the white skin part. I could be the millennial poster child of microaggressions if I wanted to be, but it can be polarizing. Race has taken an incredible swing in the last few years in terms of cultural zeitgeist and has become a very uncomfortable topic to discuss. It can be so discouraging seeing the lack of rational and basic empathy given to persons of color, and being able to effectively just listen to people, their firsthand accounts, or stories.

As an adoptee, I quickly identified as a child that I was different than my peers. Sometimes I wore it like a badge of honor. Other times it was lonely, or something to reaffirm insecurities. This rings especially true for those of us Colombians who are darker skinned. Most of us at some point have experienced the pointed looks, the mild disbelief or dismissals of opinions, the patronizing tones, and, if unlucky, the very occasional wildly ignorant comment or slur.

Despite all that, I was able eventually to develop thick skin and a more transparent understanding of what life can really be. My story would certainly be considered mild compared to others, but that doesn't devalue the experience. I'm one of many, and I know I'm not truly alone.

Growing up in comfort, my adoptive mother instilled a sensitive and creative side to my personality.I loved school and have always been curious. With my middle class comfort, I found great pleasure in the creation of arts and media. I've been an avid songwriter since barely knowing how to play my own instruments: because that lonely funny feeling as a kid was waiting to be molded into a unique story unlike most others around my immediate surroundings. At least that's the grandiose thought I had as a kid, and I'll probably continue to do so until I die, since my career path is in the music industry.

I wrote the following songs as a teenager. I chose these two songs to present here as they were the first pieces I'd ever written that addressed my adoptee experience. They mostly center on my conflicted feelings over my biological mother and my adoptive mother. Why did my biological mother give me up? What did she feel? Does she think of me? Does she want to reconnect? Another large theme is how this relates to my adoptive mother, who I hold very near and dear. She is a sensitive person, and I know that my longing and yearning for my biological mother to recognize or reconnect with me could be cause for jealousy or anguish. I love my adoptive mother, and I empathize with her, but I can't change the way I feel. Finding reconciliation in our mother-son triangle is what I try to do through my music. My adoptive family has never been big on talking or sharing deep-seated thoughts and feelings. Story telling and music, like many other art forms, is my way of expression and release, and this is the only way I can honestly, comfortably, and unapologetically relay just that. I've begun to take real steps towards finding my biological mother; and if she wants to talk and know me, I look forward to discussing these works with her in frank. Because as much as these songs are for myself and anyone else that might have a similar experience, I'd be lying if I said these songs aren't also for her.

"Take Me Home"

By myself I felt so, very far way
Lost in time or I'm just, lost in this space
It was so hard to go away
The despair of that day, so long ago

In my bedroom, down at the park
In my mind it crept, waiting in the dark
Lingering in my soul
Something I never knew for sure
I never forget those, days back then
Just waiting for it to, all make sense
Well I think I found the cure

[Chorus]
Like an infant's mind, all along the answer so pure
But when you're born to be sold it's hard to feel and to know
Where you call home
Unending love like the sky, it was here all the time
I was young, I didn't know
So much impatience, to really grow
No more lying and I'll keep trying

[Verse 2]
Growing up
The years go by
Branded in mind, fading with time
When does she sit and think of me?
Or am I some awful horrible dream?
Every night?

Even though, I'm somehow guided here
I don't blame anyone
I have no more fear
There's nothing I can change
Even if I could, I'd rather stay the same
Dear mother of mine, don't shed another tear
No matter where I go, you're always near
And that's something that won't change

Cause when you're born to be sold, it's hard to feel and to know
[Chorus]

Where you call home
Unending love like the sky, it was here all the time

I was unsteady, as a boy
Not yet ready, for so much joy
When I found home.

"She"

Twisting in my sheets, she's falling into my dreams
And now she is nothing, nothing
If I could just have that one glance, I'm sure it'd be my last
As the world would crumble into pieces
But it happens every day, since you've been away
Another lonely heart on a winding road
With nowhere to go

You're just another world away, I've always hoped you've been okay
Cause I've been so curious to know you
Lying down in my wet pillow, it's just how some things go
I know, I was just a boy and all alone

But dear woman I hope you know
My love for you still grows
No matter what I say, any given day, dear mother
If I could only say

Eric Johnson was adopted as an infant from Bogotá, Colombia, in August of 1991, by a married couple from the Park Rapids, Minnesota, area in the U.S. Eric's family relocated five years later to Fergus Falls, MN, where they finally settled in. After graduating from high school, he moved to Minneapolis and began his studies at MCTC for an audio engineering degree. Eric graduated with an AS in the Sound Arts field. For his thesis project, Eric received the highest honor in his graduating class in the form of the 2013 Cinema Excellence Award. Eric continues to write, record, and produce music and audio content. He makes his living at American Musical Supply and as a freelance audio engineer. You can find him at sleeppatternproductions.com.

The Trademark Of Adoptivehood

Yennifer Dallmann/Villa

Du bist meine Mutter,
aber ich nicht Dein Kind.
Ich bin Deine Tochter,
aber Du hast mich nicht geboren.
Du gabst mir eine Chance zu leben,
aber Du hast mir mein Leben nicht geschenkt.

You are my mother,
but I am not your child.
I am your daughter,
but you did not give birth to me.
You gave me a chance to live,
but my life was not yours to give.

Wachen bis das Licht die Schatten bricht.
Wer nicht bewacht wird, muss selbst Wache halten.
Schlafe, sagt die Sonne, Heute nicht.
Ein Tag noch.
Ein Tag noch Galgenfrist.
Die anderen Kinder sprechen Sätze und ich spreche nicht.
Neue Sprache, neues Essen, neue Menschen. Neues Ich?
Ich höre Geräusche im Vorhang.
Ich höre Lieder, die niemand mehr singt.
Werde ich einmal noch Deine Augen sehen?
Ich möchte durch den Spiegel greifen.
Bin ich der letzte Weg zurück zu Dir.

Awake, keeping watch until light scattered the shadows.
Those who are not watched over must stand for themselves.
Sleep, says the sun, not today. One day left. One more day's reprieve.
The other children speak in sentences, and I do not speak at all.
A different language, different food, different people. Different me?
I hear noises in the curtains. I hear songs no one sings anymore.
Will I ever look into your eyes again?
I would like to reach through the mirror.
Am I the last path that leads back to you.

 Yennifer Dallmann/Villa is a Cologne-based student of sustainability and design, with a main emphasis on photography and conceptual design. She was born in Medellín in 1988 and adopted by a German couple when she was around two years old. Through her work she is trying to open up dialogue about international adoption and to speak up for those adopted children who do not have words of their own yet. She is still not reunited with her birth family, but looking forward to visiting Colombia to do more art-related projects. Yennifer wants to bring the voices of origin to those places where adoptees had been sent. For further information and recent works, visit www.yvilla.de.

Looking The Truth In The Eye
Renée Sadhana

Looking the truth in the eye is a scary thing.
Looking the truth in the eye is a necessary thing.
Not looking the truth in the eye is a cowardly thing.
Yet looking the truth in the eye is a foolish thing.
Because having looked it in the eye once,
it never ever goes away again.
Ever.

Looking the truth in the eye hurts.
Looking the truth in the eye reveals things. Ugly things. Horrible
things.
Unspeakable things.
Looking the truth in the eye is a naïve thing.
Yet not knowing the truth is a wicked thing.
Not being able to look the truth in the eye is an unbearable thing.
Because you look and look—and the only thing you see
is a big fat question mark. Leaving you empty.

Looking the truth in the eye—
Looking the truth in the eye—
Looking the truth in the eye real hard—
Things are unconcealed. Things are unshrouded. Locks are broken.
Barriers are traversed. Borders are blown up.
Some get hurt. Some can't look.
Some are cause. Some are victim
of the situation.
Some are left alone
looking.

Looking the truth in the eye—who do you turn to?
Looking the truth in the eye—where do you go for shelter?
Looking the truth in the eye—can you bear that burden? For life?
Looking the truth in the eye—what will you do with the truth
that is finally yours?
Do you hide it?
Do you write it and burn it up?
Do you bury it deep down inside you—
let it eat you up alive?
Or do you tell? Tell it all? To the trees. To the wind. To the fish.
To the rocks. To the mountains. To the flowers. To the rivers.
To the oceans. To yourself. To others?
Share? Share.
Make it even more real?
How can it do more damage? Concealed or shared?
How can I prevent it
from ever happening again?
How can I
heal?

Looking the truth straight in the eye.
Looking the truth deep in the eye.
Sharing that truth
that. is. now. mine.

Renée Sadhana was adopted from Bogotá at the age of four and grew up in central Europe, where she was the youngest among her new siblings, also adoptees from different continents. She did both her BA and MA in Literature and Linguistics and directed her career towards corporate communications and charity work. At the age of 25 she reunited with her Colombian family. Five years later, she got married to a Colombian, with whom she now lives in Europe.

I Remember…
Rita Esmeralda Naranjo

I remember…

3:00 a.m., lights shining in my face with harsh words saying, "Get up, you all are coming with us." The police stood there watching us scramble to get dressed. While my brothers and I rubbed our sleepy eyes in order to make sure we weren't dreaming, we heard no words of concern or comfort. We left with no shoes on our feet.

I remember…

My father
A soul rebel
Fighting for survival
To establish a foundation strong enough to withstand the many pressures of life
Smiles and laughter were always free flowing
Awareness and worries were always going, and business was handled with no hesitation
He represented Colombian beauty and hardship

I remember…

My mother
A beautiful woman burdened with her childhood memories
Drugs were her way of trying to forget all that had happened to her
Pain and hardship always seemed to cross her path
Losing herself and running away…
I often wondered where she went…it was always hard for her to stay
Could we…her children…fuel her will to live?
We were my mother's pride and joy…I could see it in the way she smiled at us
Leaving me with numerous stories to tell

My father was killed
Bullet to the head
The killer had no respect for the dead
Or the family that would be torn apart, crumbled, and deeply
wounded

How could things have fallen apart so quickly?
Drugs and helplessness soon overwhelmed my mother
She was unable to take care of my five brothers and me any longer
Love soon became a distant memory
Warmth and security soon became a hopeless desire
Every night I cried myself to sleep
Longing and desperate to be with my family

Did anyone feel the pain that my heart was consumed with?
No will to talk or even smile
Nobody to talk to, even for just a little while
I was a little girl that carried baggage, so heavy
My cries for help were so often unheard
So many homes, more than I can remember
Always alone, no one to be my protector

Soon my sadness turned into anger and resentment
I hated the life that I had been given
Every day I reminded myself that my mother did not love me
I was convinced that I was a child that was lost and forgotten

I remember...

Years went by with no easy roads
Anger and hope were in constant argument
Why should I care about life?
I felt as though I had no reason to be alive
I had no one to help me care
Robbing, stealing, and dealing became my only means of survival
In and out of juvenile hall...child correction...child detention...
What would become of me?

Just another child thrown away...
a wondering child...
A conscious child I was
Observing and learning
Earning my way with strategy and thoughtfulness

Many events happened in such a short period of time
My mother was gone...my father was gone...lost family...
Lost culture...lost identity...
I was left to take care of myself
I had no fear...heart on fire...mind racing...many questions...
Needing answers...
Overwhelmed...I had almost fully given up on life...my life...

At 15 years old I experienced another major life event that would
change my life forever
Young girl I was...mother to be...how could this be?
While I was pregnant I was always in my head
I realized that I determined the life of the child I was soon to have
My plan of action...I was going to find a way
What am I going to do? How am I going to do it? Where?
With what help?

Every step I took was fueled by this determination
My daughter was not going to feel the way that I felt
She was not going to have to feel alone
Without a mother constantly there
I was going to be there to kiss her and tuck her in at night
I was going to listen when she had something to say
I was going to care when and why she experienced heartache
I was also going to break the cycle of drug abuse and violence
And restore our culture...heal from trauma...relearn our history...
The next few years were filled with difficulty and struggle
Very few thought that I was capable or even able
Struggles and hardship were overcome, and surprising achievements
fought through to shine
These accomplishments were mine...for us...

I graduated from high school with my diploma
With strong willed motivation
Blessed with my daughter...her little face was my inspiration
Pushed on to get my AA
Couldn't, wouldn't stop there...got my BA
Wanted more tools to fight injustice...then received my MA
Representing less than 1% of people like me...
One who grew up in foster care...to make it this far
Is this fair?
Families wanted me...maybe adoption?
Facing abuse...I lost this option
Proud of me...proud of us...where are we?
Years of involvement in our community...believing in us...our future
Significant because we are one of many

Holding on...

Working so hard to raise my beautiful family inspiring me to be
all that I can be
Wanting to build, create, and sustain a life that is free
I have lost so much but fully cherish all that I have
My children...my crew...guiding and motivating everything that I do
Trainer...Professor...
Beading...braiding...
Organizing...cleaning...
This is my life...I stand up with the utmost warrior mama pride!
Doing my best beyond words

I dream of...

A happy and stable life...all life...my life...
Those that are around me and from a distance
We are alive
Greatness lives in us
Complex, simple and beautiful
I am a builder...
I want to contribute the best that I can to life by being true to me

The loving and caring me
The tired and exhausted courageous me
The creative and wise sister in me
The mama and wife in me...the past, present, and future in me
I will stay true through my last days

I'm still alive...I want to live...be happy
I am one of many...
There is power and hope in that...

 Rita Esmeralda Naranjo is a dedicated and determined mother and community member who has passionately pursued her personal and professional goals by striving to be an active learner and life participant. Rita's Colombian father was assassinated when she was four years old due to his involvement in drug trafficking. Rita's mother also struggled with drug addiction and was not able to care for Rita and her three brothers; all four children were taken, separated from their mother, and became wards of the state. Rita experienced abuse in potential adoptive homes but never received a permanent home/family. Rita refused to give up or forget where she came from and fought to overcome the obstacles of life with a mission and vision of creating a better life for herself, family, and community.

In 2004, Rita earned her BA in Social Work with a minor in Anthropology from San Diego State University. Then, in 2013, she earned her MA in Applied Sociological Practice from California State University, San Marcos.

Although she never found a permanent home, she has found a community of *Colombianos* that have helped her grow, heal, and stay connected to those that share a common origin and struggle with loss and separation from culture/identity. Rita's goal is to continue to support efforts that make the system of adoption and foster care better for youth, families, caregivers, and child welfare professionals.

How A Pancake Restaurant Taught
Me About Race

Abby Forero-Hilty

Introduction

I was around six years old, living with my divorced adoptive mother
(who I will refer to here as "my mother", as opposed to "*mi mamá*" for
my natural mother) in an apartment complex in a suburb of NYC,
when I first consciously remember race being an issue for me. At the
time, I didn't grasp that I was struggling with my own racial identity—
something I would continue to struggle with right up through my late
thirties—but I knew that something was very wrong. I had a deep
loneliness and longing inside of me that went beyond the daily
yearning for *mi mamá*: It was the need to be with other brown
children and children of color.

Pancakes and Race

It's raining. And there's a cockroach in my radio. Inside my radio!
How'd it get in there? Why is it sitting right there, on the blue needle
that points to the station? There's nothing to eat in a radio, not even
for a cockroach. Maybe if I turn the dial really fast back and forth I can
shake it loose...

"Sweetheart?"
"Yeah, Mom?"
"Do you want to go to I-HOP today?"
"What's 'I-HOP'?"
"It's a pancake restaurant."
"Oh. Why do they call it I-HOP?"
"It stands for 'International House Of Pancakes.'"
"Yes, yes, I wanna go!!"

Who cares about a dumb cockroach! "International." Did she say,
"international?"
Oh, then there must be kids from all over the world there! Maybe even
other kids from Colombia! Africa! India! China! Alaska! Other kids like
me who are from somewhere else, somewhere "international." I bet

they have flags from all the countries of the world hanging all over the restaurant, and kids with eyes and skin of every color, all speaking different languages! So many kids sitting at the tables, eating pancakes, and wearing clothes with bright colors! I cannot believe she is taking me to a place like this. Finally!!!!

By the time we parked the car in front of the restaurant, I was so excited I was practically panting like a dog. As I pushed the blue handle on the glass door of the restaurant, I looked around for the kids from all those countries, but there were none. All I saw were the same people I always saw on the streets, in our home, in my class at school, in our neighborhood. No colorful clothes, no brown skin, no black hair, no different languages. There was no one there who looked like me. No flags were hanging on the walls.

I thought she said "international?"

"Why aren't you eating your pancakes, Honey?"
"I don't know. I guess I'm not hungry, Mom."

***

I didn't cry or explain to her why I had lost my appetite, mainly because I wasn't able to put the enormity of my disappointment—and the reason(s) for it—into words at that age. What I did do was slowly replay, over and over for years, what happened the moment I pushed open the glass door of the restaurant, but with the outcome I had been hoping for and expecting...

***

That's a funny color blue for a door handle. Oh! Look at all of the kids inside. Wow!! This door is heavy, but I have to get in! Did it. Phew. Hey, there are no grown-ups here! Even Mom has disappeared. Yes!! I can't even see the ceiling there are so many little flags from every country covering it!

Mmmmm, I can smell soft butter, hot pancakes, and maple syrup! I love those smells. My fingers are gonna get so sticky 'cause there are no forks or knives on the tables!!

Where are all the booths like in other restaurants? Doesn't matter! The tables are so long there is room for all the food and all the kids. Everyone is smiling and talking and laughing and eating with their hands. This is my new favorite restaurant! I wanna sit over there, between the black boy and the girl with light brown skin and black hair just like mine. Her dress is so pretty—bright pink and green and white and blue and orange and purple and red. I think she has every color in the world on her dress! Oh, and look at her! Maybe she's from China. And look at that boy. His skin is a different dark brown. There's even a kid with white skin and a Yankees baseball hat! I guess he's from New York. All the kids in the world are here! And I'm here too! It feels so good to be here. Right now, I really am Colombian.

Today is the best day of my life.

Love and Race: Two Sides of the Same Coin

"Adoption" and "adopted" were not secret or taboo words in my home growing up as a child. In fact, I have always known I am adopted from Colombia, although I have no specific memory of having been told.

On the other hand, there were also no books about Colombia in our home. No attempt was made by my parents—or anyone else in my family—to learn Spanish; no Colombian food was cooked; no Colombian holidays were known about let alone celebrated. There were no Colombians, or Latinos of any kind, in my parents' circle of friends (which, of course, translated into my social world as well). We never watched films about Colombia, never listened to Colombian music, and the topic of travelling to Colombia (so I could see where I came from!) was never discussed in our home. Not even once.

At the time of my adoption, my parents were still married despite the facts that my father was a drug addict, my mother was ill-equipped to deal with his problems and those of a collapsing marriage, and their newly adopted infant had uncorrected congenital dislocated hips and she refused to drink more formula than was absolutely necessary to survive.

As an adult, I now know that these were most likely contributory reasons why my parents had fully bought into and been lulled and brainwashed by the adoption industry's "wisdom" of the day. It was the mid-1970s and, in general, in the USA, adoptive parents of transracial, transnational adoptees were told, "love is enough." They were encouraged to simply treat their adopted child as if they were their own—no different from any biological child that they theoretically would have produced. However, treating a brown child as if they were a white child—when indeed they are not—, and surrounding them with exclusively white culture and white people, is tantamount to denying that child's very being. It is denying reality.

I carried a lot of unspoken sadness, anger, confusion, jealousy, fear, and shame because of this way of thinking and parenting. Yet I learned. I learned to feel safer and more comfortable around the dominant white culture I was raised in; that white folks were friends, family, and coworkers, while people of color were not; that English was the only language spoken by our friends, family, and coworkers. But every coin has two sides. So, in turn, I also learned to feel uncomfortable around other Latinos and people of color; that our interactions with people of color were limited to those in service positions—the occasional babysitter, the bank teller, or the woman at the supermarket checkout line; that Spanish was not important enough to be learned.

I don't blame my parents as they were merely following the status quo of the adoption industry at the time. However, I still find it next to impossible to understand how such a system of "thought" could be deemed by anyone to be "in the child's best interest," regardless of what "experts" and well-meaning lay people may have said.

A Blank Slate That Isn't Blank Can't Be Erased

Looking back, I realize now that I coped with this complete lack of cultural, racial, and ethnic mirroring by spending many hours creating, reliving, and expanding on fantasies, inspired by real events, at different time points in my life. I wasn't a "blank slate" from which my entire ancestry, family, race, ethnicity, language, and history could be removed with the swipe of an old blackboard eraser without a trace, only to be replaced by new names and a heritage that belonged to my adoptive parents' potential biological child that never was to be. I was a baby, and, like any other person, my blood carried millennia of genetic information in the form of DNA, while my brain held memories of nine months in *mi mamá's* body and two months of the smells, sounds, and climate of my Colombian homeland before I was adopted and taken to grow up in New York City suburbia.

Not knowing where or whom I came from led to problems figuring out who I was for decades. With the passing of years, the help of therapy, and the gaining of maturity, I have found the courage and support I needed to walk away from the person I was supposed to be and towards the person I really am. As a proud Colombian woman of color who's been through the hell of living most of her life in an identity vacuum and the subsequent profound struggle to finally embrace and fight to regain her native-born culture, language, family, and ancestry, I know that love is important, but it isn't enough. I even go so far as to suggest that the importance of race and ethnicity is equivalent to that of love in terms of developing a healthy sense of identity. Racial and ethnic validation, respect, mirroring, and the celebration of the adopted child's race and ethnicity as well as teachings on how to navigate within the child's race are as essential as unconditional love. Though I had to grow up without any such racial and ethnic guidance or recognition, I work every day to make sure that I'm doing things differently for my children.

I have no desire to erase any people from or moments shared with my adoptive family. They are part of who I am and I love them. On the other hand, I know that no human being is a blank slate. A person's identity cannot simply be replaced with a new one without serious consequences. Although we are all individuals, we are each also the genetic culmination of every one of our ancestors who came before us.

Our ancestors call to us through our DNA. Even though they may be long gone or out of reach, we can hear them when we talk and laugh, and we can see them in the features of our faces, in the lines and curves of our bodies, and in the way we move. We are canvases partially painted by the ancient brushstrokes of our ancestors. There is nothing blank about that.

Abby Forero-Hilty was adopted from Bogotá at the age of two months and grew up in a small suburb of New York City. She received her BS in Human Biology from the State University of New York at Albany and her MS in Medical Anthropology from University College London. In 1998, Abby moved to Switzerland, where she lives with her life partner and their two children. She currently works in the pharmaceutical industry, collaborating with scientists and health authorities worldwide to bring new oncology drugs to patients in need. Abby enjoys hiking, dancing, writing, travelling, exploring nature, and being with beloved friends and family. She has been reunited with her *familia* in Colombia since March 2012. This is her first book.

A Sense Of Lost
Paul Aboulafia (Saul Rodriguez)

Her spry brown Colombian eyes had always been deceptive. But if anyone looked below them one would see dark bags underneath—the two mounds of puffy gloom told another story.

On this spring day, her older brother sent her a Facebook message. Above the message was a disclaimer addressed directly to Vera. It stated the following: I am sorry sister, but I can no longer live my life keeping our childhood abuse a secret.

As she read the message, each word felt like tiny daggers pricking into her back. Facing the computer, absorbing the final word along with the glow from the monitor, her body slowly sank into the uncomfortable wooden chair. Her shoulders dropped, while she tried mindlessly to press her chin into the top part of her chest. With downcast eyes, she stared at the patterns on her orange, blue, and white plaid dress.

Outside, it was a hot spring day: blue skies and sunshine. Inside it was gray and smelled like musky old books and body odor.

Sitting there, she did not notice that her 30-minute computer session was almost over at the Brooklyn Public Library. She felt betrayed, hurt, angry, and relieved. She refused to relive the memories of being beaten, of having her hair ripped out of her head, or of being groped and worse. She just sat there quiet and motionless, fighting back tears. Every time a sob tried to come up into her throat, she would swallow it back down with a gulp of saliva.

Her skin was light brown and her face still looked young despite all the years of hiding behind a mask of denial and abuse. By now, her eyes were fixed on a bookshelf a few feet behind her computer screen. Her eyes indicated a sense of loss. The contents of the message exposed one simple truth that her family's dirty secret was out.

For the first time in her 34 years of life, Vera lost control over who knew what had happened to her.

The placid look in her eyes was gone and replaced with emptiness. Despite this, she was filled with a hellish delight. She was free from hiding. This freedom, however, only brought her closer to a life filled with embarrassment, for Peter sent copies of this message to every mutually known friend and relative on her and his Facebook accounts.

When the computer session was over, she stood up and walked out of the library and toward the nearest pharmacy. With her big sullen brown eyes, she stared at a shelf full of bottles filled with sleeping pills.

Paul Aboulafia (Saul Rodriguez) was adopted from Bucaramanga, Colombia, at the age of three. He was raised in Brooklyn, New York. Later in life, he earned a BA in Political Science from SUNY New Paltz and then two MAs, one in Political Science and the other in Education from the City University of New York (CUNY). For over 18 years, he was a public school educator for the New York Department of Education and for the City University of New York (CUNY). In 2016, Paul along with his wife and two sons moved to France.

La Pared (The Wall)
Yvonne M. Roach (Maria Velasquez)

There is a wall in my life. It is one wall with different façades; at least this is how it feels for me, with the central themes of being disconnected to my first language and culture, and how it hindered me early on in childhood. My wall and what it has grown to become in my life today was not recognizable until adulthood. As a young child I sensed an ominous presence, which made me feel separate from the world around me. I can recall happily playing outside and stopping suddenly, sensing an indescribable presence. I did not feel fear, but I did become keenly aware of not fitting in somehow. The whole world would move on by. I was unable to move or be part of what blocked me. The world that moved was the world in the United States. How could that be when I loved my family? I now recognize this sensation as a wall that literally separates me from my origins, from my view and understanding.

Within me, my wall evokes strong feelings in the core of my body of something thick, like a redwood tree trunk that must be expelled from my body. When this redwood tree trunk rises through my core, emotions I cannot describe rush out, as one forceful, physical vomitus mass. Externally, my wall takes the form of an invisible boundary that I try to pass through but which holds me back. It's as if I am challenged to pass through a heavy industrial gel that reaches upwards and downwards, without end. The efforts I must exert are exhaustive. As an adoptee from Colombia, my life with my adoptive family was beautiful and without difficulties, yet I know I was not of their culture and I was without mine! As a Colombian adoptee in a Caucasian household, I knew nothing of my Colombian culture, my people with their own long histories and language.

All through my life when I reflect upon moments, there have been times I was looking at my wall. There have been times that the wall surrounded me and cut me off from whatever lay on the other side. As a small child I was blocked from understanding things as quickly as my peers. To this day, I cannot understand why it took me an exorbitant amount of time to catch on to meanings of things. I struggled academically in school through the third grade.

Other times, like in my adult years, I could not gain a connection to my first culture and language. Though I had many friends from different countries who spoke my first language, I was not and still have not been able to tear down this façade of the wall that leaves me out. It was and remains enormous enough to block out considerations of what might lie on the other side.

Describing my wall means the admission and understanding today that my life in the United States is on one side of the wall, making me an adoptee, while on the other side of my wall is my life as a *Colombiana*—and I do not remember it! I have zero connection to it and I cannot hold on to any of these Colombian roots! I am ready to face what seems to be unknown to me, though as I think about the pursuit of my origins, I feel the wall becoming taller and thicker, an impenetrable barrier. What is it that my inner self feels the need to protect me from?

A duality exists in my life. I am a high functioning adult and living a full life with my family, friends, and career. I have the freedom to choose well and to give! However, when I turn to my wall, there it is...the existing feelings that there is a part of my life that could grow but is not accessible to me. Am I stunted in one area of my life? How can I fill in the blank lines?

What pains me the most is that I lost my language. There is an enormous block in regaining my first language. *Español* is my first language, replaced with English, and English has become my "new" first language. This is the façade of the wall that hurts the most; it stings. Over the course of this last year, I encountered many physical symptoms that seemed to be a medical problem, only to find out that the deep inner hurt from being relinquished through the adoption process manifested into outward physical symptoms, making me quite ill. My primary care physician was quick to notice that I needed to seek counseling to address the trauma my body remembers though my mind does not.

Through my counseling sessions, I found the courage to begin lessons in Spanish. During the time with my instructor, I could not mouth one word in Spanish. My mouth would not move to form the words. I was mortified because I am normally unafraid of speaking and sharing how I feel, but what occurred during this language lesson hurt deeply. Deep within the core of my soul came out as a vomitus cry and wail, "I lost my language!" I felt such agony over this loss.

Español would grant me access to my people and the discovery of my people. *Español* would allow me to use my skills to help others within my culture. The enormity of losing my first language and trying to recapture it overwhelms me to the point of numbness, because it is easier to not embrace the reality of this struggle. I am filled with frustration at my many efforts to learn...I must relearn my language of origin. Humiliating! Yet, I know with all logic and heart it is not my fault. I could vomitus cry out a wail of outrage, yet again! I will not give up, yet the process of overcoming or even knocking down this wall to reveal the internal trauma seems daunting and exhausting. I find zero comfort in having an enormous limitation, because I know now that this wall is not healthy and prevents me from living my life to its fullest. Is that not what we all strive towards?

When a rooted plant is plucked from the ground, the roots lack the much-needed rich nutrients and moisture of the soil. Colombia is rich soil filled with bountiful nutrients of language, food, history, people, and vibrancy! My roots have not been in Colombia for well over 40 years...they feel nothing. I feel nothing when I think of myself as a *Colombiana*. I have zero connection! I can only view this disconnection, as if I am looking at someone else's life, with enormous feelings of empathy. It is like I must advocate for this woman and, despite the challenges, I will fight to ensure this woman finds a connection to her Colombian roots!

Yvonne Marie Roach (Maria Velasquez) was adopted from Bogotá at nine months of age and began her childhood in the small town of Pepperrell, Massachusetts. Eventually, the family moved to Ocala, Florida, where she resides currently with her husband of 22 years; they have one son together, age 19. Yvonne earned her BA in Business Administration, worked in the social services industry, and is now in the manufacturing industry as a Human Resources professional.

Yvonne enjoys being outdoors, whether running, camping or just being with her family and three dogs. She has searched for her first family with the help of an investigator and one day, a possible reunion may occur.

It Took Seven Years To Find My Birthmother; Now What?

Claire Mielke Rogness

"Now I lay me down to sleep, I pray the Lord my soul to keep. Guide and watch me through the night and wake me with the morning light. God bless Mommy, Daddy, Johnny, aunties and uncles, grandmas and grandpas, and my birthmom in Colombia." This is a prayer I would say every night before I went to bed. My adoptive parents, which from now on I will refer to as my parents, always included my birthmom when we prayed. My parents were always very open with me regarding my adoption story and my mom always told me how much she wanted to meet my birthmom someday and thank her for giving her the opportunity to be a mom and to have a daughter.

Throughout my childhood, I always dreamt of finding my birthmom one day. It always fascinated me to know that we would always think of each other at the same time each year on my birthday, October 5th. I wanted to know if I looked like her. I wanted to let her know I was not mad at her for putting me up for adoption. I wanted to know my medical history. I wanted to know more about my biological siblings and how many I had. I wanted to know more about my biological father. I wanted to know: Why???

As my high school and college years went by, I didn't think much about finding my birthmom. It seemed like an impossible endeavor. However, when I became engaged in 2006 I dreamt of my birthmom being at my wedding. It was in 2006 that I started the search for my Colombian family. Facebook was fairly new in 2006, so it didn't help me at all in the search. My mom loves to meet new people, and, in 2006, while traveling by plane, she met a Colombian woman who attempted to help us find my birthmother. We had the address where I was born, and my mom gave it to her. This lady went to the house at this address and an old woman answered the door and then shut it immediately, another dead end. I was married in 2007 and the dream of having my birthmom at the wedding folded. I felt like "it" would never happen. It just seemed too hard to ever find her. I was sad and angry all at once.

I once again went on with my life thinking that I would never be reunited with my birth family. It wasn't until after having my first child that I knew I needed to find her. Becoming a mother gave me a sense of what she must have gone through to give me up for adoption. I needed to tell her I was safe, healthy, and happy. I wanted to let her know I wasn't mad at her and that I acknowledge that she had to make tough decision based on love. As I looked at my four-week-old son in my arms, I realized that the decision my birthmom made to put me up for adoption must have been one of the hardest, most difficult things she had ever done.

I had been told that my birthmother attempted to care for me for a month, but I had two older siblings she took care of and she just couldn't keep me healthy. She turned me over to ICBF (*Instituto Colombiano de Bienestar Familiar*; governmental institution that handles adoptions in Colombia) when I was one month old. I get choked up to think of how hard it must have been for her. I feel sad for the baby I once was. How hard it must have been on the both of us. The physical bond that she formed with me was now broken forever. She had to hope and pray that I went to a loving couple who would love and raise me.

In 2013, I contacted a journalist in Neiva who helped me come up with a newspaper article about my adoption and included my birthmother's name, Maria Elena Cuellar. Unfortunately, we received no leads with this article. It wasn't until I joined a Facebook group for Colombian adoptees and their families that I was put in contact with Gyna who runs *Colombia Tu Pais*, an organization that reunites adoptees and their biological families. Within two weeks, Gyna had located my Colombian family. I could not believe it. I was so emotional to find that both of my birth parents are alive and in addition that I have nine half-brothers and sisters and one full sister. I spent many nights meeting and talking to all my siblings and birth parents on Skype and Facebook. No one spoke English, so I spoke Spanish. I had studied Spanish in college because I wanted to be able to communicate with my birth family if I ever did find them. Speaking Spanish definitely helped with communicating with everyone.

However, I was an emotional wreck because I was pregnant with my second child and my brain hurt so badly from speaking Spanish every night. I felt guilty that I wasn't spending time with my husband and my son. I was very angry and sad that I didn't get to grow up with my full sister, Norma. However, she told me that as much as she too wished I had grown up with her she was so happy that I didn't because she had a hard life mostly because she was physically and mentally abused along with many of her siblings. Her relationship with her dad was absent and it was hit or miss with her mom. She moved to Mexico as soon as she turned 17. I had and still have mixed emotions about finding my birth family. I don't feel like I missed out on much except for growing up with my siblings. My mom and I are so close that I have no feelings towards my birthmother in terms of wishing I had been raised by her. I know that sounds cold, but I love my mom and it makes me sad to know that I wouldn't have had her love and support if I had stayed in Colombia. Despite my conflicting feelings, after a year of getting to know my family over the Internet, I decided it was time to meet everyone.

On September 10, 2014, my husband, my parents, and I flew to Neiva and then drove four hours to a town called Pitalito. We spent 10 days meeting everyone. I can't even describe my feelings and how emotional I was. Hugging my birthmom at the airport for the first time was so beautiful. The woman who brought me into this world was now in my arms. The woman I had prayed for so many times was REAL. She was there. We both cried. I cannot imagine what she was thinking. The baby girl she had kissed goodbye 33 years prior was now in her arms again. The mother, who had known nothing about where her daughter had been or who had raised her, was finally able to hold her baby girl—who was now a woman!—in her arms again. I told my birthmom that I was not mad at her at all. This made her so happy. She said she had had no idea where I had been living or if I had been safe for all these years. I thanked her for my life. It was amazing to meet my Colombian siblings. I felt like I connected with my siblings more than my birth parents.

One thing I did learn is that I was the only one put up for adoption. I do have one half-sister that was adopted by her uncle, so she stayed within the family.

I have been having a hard time understanding why I am the only one who was put up for adoption and completely left the continent. Why me? I truly believe everything happens for a reason. I am not quite sure yet what that reason is.

 Claire Mielke Rogness was adopted from Neiva, Colombia, at the age of four months. She grew up in small suburb of St. Paul, Minnesota. She received her BS in Biology and Spanish at Gustavus Adolphus College in Southern Minnesota. She then went on and obtained her doctorate of dental surgery at the University of Minnesota Dental School. Following that, Claire did a two-year residency program specializing in pediatric dentistry at Children's Hospital Colorado. Claire was reunited with her birth family in the fall of 2013. She has attempted to help her sister come visit on a tourist visa, but her sister was rejected at Atlanta customs. Claire then tried to get her visa again two years later but they did not re-issue it to her. Currently, Claire lives in Minnesota with her husband and three kids—and one on the way. She is a pediatric dentist in Maplewood and Stillwater, Minnesota.

Claire enjoys being surrounded by her family and friends, working out, traveling, and advocating for children's dental health.

The Emotional Struggles
Jennifer Beth Capeless

Excited, in disbelief, anxious, happy; so many other feelings that I can't put my finger on just one. I am so overwhelmed with emotions that my head feels like it cannot function properly. And this is only the beginning. I know there will be more to come and all of them will grow stronger. I just hope I'll be able to handle them. This isn't easy for me and I know it's not for anyone else. I do hope I can keep it together enough so I don't hurt anyone's feelings. This will continue to be an incredible journey and I'm thankful to have it.

I feel like my first trip back will be incredibly emotional for me. I've always wanted to go to Colombia, to find my biological mother and soak in the country because my adoption papers could only tell me so much. I knew my birth name and that of my biological mother, her history (as in why she chose to give me up), all of my birth information, and I had the documentation of my biological mother giving up her rights as a parent. I had yearned to know who my biological mother was and from whom I had inherited some of my physical, emotional, and mental attributes. I wanted to know who my biological mother was even more than I already did because my adoption papers were so thorough and my parents had a pretty good sense of the type of woman she was and ALWAYS spoke of her positively, even though they had never met her. I wanted to know where I would have "naturally" fit in. I know that may sound as though I was not happy or loved by my family but that's not what I mean. To know where you come from and where certain attributes come from, which make you who you are, are questions many adoptees have but which cannot be answered until they can make a connection with their biological family and learn about their history. And a part of learning about one's history is learning about the country that they come from. I had always thought about the country too. In my mind, Colombia was beautifully green and full of life. So many colors, smells, and sounds that at first would feel so foreign but would so quickly make me feel like home. But all of these fluffy feelings and expectations have been pushed aside and even crushed at times because of the country's negative reputation.

My first trip back to Colombia since I was adopted as a baby can sometimes feel long overdue. Although I only found my biological family four years ago, I've known ever since I was young that I'd go Colombia to meet my biological family. I say when I was young because I do not have a specific memory of my parents telling me I was adopted. My parents were very open with me about my adoption and what it meant to be adopted. My mom was also adopted, which in hindsight comforted me because there was never a feeling of me being different from my parents or other siblings even though there is an undeniable difference between all of us. However, despite my strong desire to find my biological family, it has not been very easy to follow through with it. My parents, who have loved me since the day they found out I was to be their daughter, have always been very overprotective. As a child, I never knew anything different and was very innocent. Yet as I grew older I learned and found out not all parents were like mine. When I was a teenager I hated it but I learned that if I did not listen to them there were consequences. But they were just looking out for me and I have pretty much always listened to my parents and did what they wanted.

So when I told them and my boyfriend at the time that I had found my biological mother, and that I had told her I would go to Colombia the first chance I could, my family were not happy with that proposition, to say the least. My parents told me not to go and my boyfriend didn't want to go with me. They said, "You don't know if she's really your biological mother. How can you be 100% sure? You don't know anything about your biological family; how can you trust them? Give it time," they said, "to get to know her." Despite my best efforts to push back and tell them I believed I was her biological daughter and how I am not a person who goes back on my word, they did not change their minds. It was very hurtful and disappointing at the time that they did not support me visiting my biological family when I first found them. I was extremely frustrated and when I get very upset I have to journal how I feel. It not only lets me say how I feel in the moment but also makes me feel validated at the time for feeling the way I do. Even though I was not able to meet my biological mother when I wanted to, I knew at least she was available for me to talk to and we were still able to establish a connection. I continued to talk to my new family and learn about them and catch them up with me and my life.

Then, finally, after over a year of talking with my new family, my parents were open to the idea of me visiting with my biological mother and they invited her to our yearly family vacation on a Spanish-speaking island. Although I was upset that it had taken so long for a reunion to happen, I was incredibly excited and eager to help my biological mother prepare for her trip to reunite with me.

After weeks of planning our reunion I finally heard that my biological mother, Blanca, was approved for her visa so we could meet up! I was so overwhelmed that I cried for joy and out of disbelief. The biggest wish I'd ever had was finally becoming a reality; it all hit me at once, and my emotions just took over. Meeting my biological mother was something I'd always wanted but had seemed so unattainable. I couldn't believe it was actually happening! And I kept thinking, "I'll really believe it when it actually happens—when I actually see/meet her in person." Finally, the day came that Blanca and I were going to meet each other! My half-brother, Samuel, (Blanca's son) was giving me Blanca's travel updates and by then it was finally sinking in, how close were to meeting. I remember writing her name on a welcome wipe board for her, so she would know where I was, and thinking, "It's finally here." My parents, fiancé, sisters, brother, and a few family friends piled into a taxi van to pick up Blanca.

Once we got to the airport, I remember having a hard time figuring out where I was going to be able to meet her. We finally found the exit for the incoming passengers, which was visible through clear glass. I was happy that we were able to see each other even sooner than at the exit door. Waiting for her to arrive felt like an eternity. But I finally saw her through the glass wall and she saw me. My body took over and I began hyperventilating and crying uncontrollably. As I was crying I saw *mi mamá*, Blanca, standing where she first saw me, and she was crying too. After that my sense of time seems to have been lost. I remember Blanca began moving closer to me, going down the escalator while I kept crying. We finally embraced in the exit doorway, crying into each other's arms. After a few minutes of blocking a few passengers exiting the doorway, we moved out into the hallway where I began introducing *mi mamá* to my family. We then left the airport to check *Mamá* into her hotel room and had dinner.

The next morning, I woke up early and walked down to *mi mamá's* room so she could get ready for the day and have breakfast. Since I do not speak Spanish fluently, speaking with her one on one was difficult. But a couple of our family friends who were with us did speak Spanish and helped us communicate. The next few days we visited with each other and spoke about past and present events. Talking so freely helped us understand one another and connect. It was truly amazing how loving she was with me from the moment we met and throughout our trip together. Wherever we went she held my hand, and, whenever she could, she held me. I remember one day we were walking around the hotel and a young woman made a smart comment to someone she was with like, "Oh, we better hold hands. We don't want to be apart." At the time I was so enraged; how can strangers be so rude?! I wanted to say something back like 'Well how about you wait 27 years to meet your biological mother and you have some stranger judge you on how you're with your mother!' But I did not want to act poorly in front of *mi mamá*, so I held my tongue.

One topic that we did discuss on our trip was my upcoming wedding! I wanted not only *mi mamá* to come but the rest of my Colombian family as well. Before Blanca left I packed her suitcase with sweaters for all my Colombian family members because November in Massachusetts is cold—a hell of a lot colder than what they are all used to. Although we were leaving each other with sadness in our hearts, we were very excited about meeting up next year for my wedding.

After almost a year of planning for my wedding, I learned *mi mamá* was granted a U.S. visa valid for 10 years. The year before I had sent money over for *mi mamá* and my sister to get their passports and visas, but only *mi mamá* had her visa approved because the government said that my sister did not have any legal ties to Colombia to ensure that she would return and not become an illegal citizen of the U.S. The rest of my family was hesitant to apply for the visas and waste the money I had sent to them for the application process. Although I understood why they did not want to apply I was disheartened they were not coming. However, I was thrilled that *mi mamá* was able to come. I prepared for the wedding and Blanca's arrival as much as possible before she came so I would be able to spend as much time with her as I could once she arrived. When she came we had a couple of days by ourselves, in which time I tried my best to prepare her for the days ahead. It was very special for me to have her with me on my wedding day and I know she felt the same. We shared a few moments together on my wedding day that I cherish dearly. The wedding was beautiful and was even more special with *mi mamá* there with me.

Despite how well I thought the visit went, I believe the cultural differences were very difficult for her on top of the limited amount of people that she was able to communicate with (because of the language barrier). I did not realize how many aspects of my life would differ from *mi mamá's*, and how hard it would be for her to understand me and my family culturally. I think as people we get caught up in just living how we are used to and do not stop and think how differently we live compared to others, whether it be our friends, neighbors, or family, let alone people in other nations. So it was disappointing for me to see how bringing *mi mamá* here did not just make her happy but also upset her at times. The night before she left she was singing, "*Voy a Colombia. Voy a Colombia.*" (I am going to Colombia. I am going to Colombia). It was sad to hear her singing so happily but I knew it was partially my fault for not being with her the entire time.

On the drive back to my house from my parents' house, she asked if I wanted to go to Colombia one day. I said of course I did. I told her that I wanted to so badly but that I wanted to respect my husband and my family and that I needed to wait. I'm not completely sure if she understood that. How could I possibly explain to her in my three-year-old-child Spanish how complicated this is for me? Our language barrier can be very challenging at times but I feel as though the way we speak and the sincerity of our words speak more to one another than the words we choose. My family, who loves me and supports me, is more afraid of guerillas and kidnappers than focusing on the wonderful and beautiful connection I'd be making with my biological family. With the little explanation I could give to *Mamá*, she said she understood and hoped that maybe within the next three years I could come. I just said all I could, "Yes!"

When we got home I tried to teach her some words in English by pointing to everyday objects. We then joined my husband, John, in the living room and watched American football. John and I began teaching her about the game, which she seemed to find interesting but cringed at each tackle and hit the players took on their opponent. That night I felt like we'd been connecting and the stage of feeling each other out was gone. We were both comfortable with each other and could enjoy each other's company and be ourselves. I was disappointed that the next morning she was leaving, just as I felt we were connecting. The next morning my husband had to take *Mamá* to the airport because I had been very sick the night before and had only had two hours of sleep. We embraced each other and said our goodbyes. I wanted to give her a date when we'd see each other again but I had no clue when that would be.

So, a year and seven months later I booked my first trip to Colombia. I had so many feelings towards the trip but I did not have a lot of time to dwell on them because my life was so busy. My grandfather was very sick, my work was incredibly busy, and we were getting ready for our trip as well as attending other family events. My husband was having a hard time sleeping a couple weeks leading up to our trip because he was worried about our safety. And my mom was incredibly worried that when we would leave Colombia, Immigration would give me a hard time because I did not have a Colombian passport. Although these were my family's feelings at the time, I could not help but worry with them because we are so close and when they are upset, I too get upset. Despite my best efforts to console my loved ones that everything was going to be okay throughout the trip, I could not change the way they felt; all I could do was show I love them by comforting them as much as I could.

Only when I got on the plane to start my trip to Colombia did I have time to really think about how momentous the trip was going to be for me. I would not only be seeing my family but I would be able to experience a small part of the country with the people and culture. I felt that there were so many possibilities to this trip and what it could bring. All I truly wanted was for all of us to have a great time and have amazing memories afterwards.

I hoped my mom and John would be comfortable enough to go out with my family and me outside of the hotel. I was already mentally prepared that I would be going out with my family by myself since my mom and John made it very clear that they were uncomfortable walking around in Colombia. But in my mind I did not quite understand that because my Colombian family are my loves. I brought them into my life and they brought me into theirs. Although we do not know each other inside-out like my adoptive family and my husband do, we love each other and would feel completely horrible if we ever unknowingly hurt each other. But I guess my adoptive family and husband did not understand that. They did not know the love that had formed between myself and my Colombian family because they are not in our shoes. I had to remind myself that everything I had experienced with my Colombian family, my adoptive family and husband had not been a part of.

Because of that I have come to believe that neither I, nor my mom, nor John should make each other feel as though our personal feelings are wrong. We all feel true to our feelings and are expressing them as honestly to one another as possible. And with that we have to just be supportive of each other no matter how hard it is to completely understand how the opposite side is feeling. No matter how we may have felt during or after arguments/misunderstandings, we had to remind ourselves that we were all going on the trip out of love. I was traveling to Colombia to connect with my biological family and to learn about my native culture and country. My husband and mom were going out of love and support for me and out of the love for my biological family as well.

Once we began flying over some mountains near Bogotá, I finally saw the beautiful greenery that I knew I would fall in love with. I was in such awe of the view from my airplane window that I almost forgot to take pictures. When we were in El Dorado airport I felt a bit uncomfortable because it was so foreign and I cannot speak Spanish fluently, but I was so happy to be there especially because it felt so warm and inviting. Just one more flight and we'd be with my family! It felt so unbelievable to me.

We were finally in Pereira! My brother, sister, and her fiancé were anxiously waiting for us outside of the airport. I remember her texting me while we were getting our bags and asking if we were coming out of the airport. We walked outside into a crowd of people mostly wearing Colombian *fútbol* jerseys (because there was a game that night), and I was having such a hard time finding my siblings. My eyes moved towards the outside ring of people and finally found my sister's fiancé, Hector. He saw me too and told my sister, Luisa, and Samuel, where we were. All of a sudden I nearly got knocked over by my sister's running embrace. Again, I was overwhelmed with happiness that I don't quite remember how long we all were hugging one another. I just know we all hugged each other with plenty of tears. My family then helped my mom, John, and me to our taxi to our hotel. It was incredible! How they took care of us so warmly. My mom and John were amazed by my family immediately. I was so happy and proud to hear that. All there was left to do was surprise *mi mamá*, *mi abuela* (grandma), and my stepfather, Luis.

A couple of hours later my sister texted me that all my family was right outside of the hotel. I walked out of the hotel quietly and, as I was approaching, *mi abuela* saw me first and was awestruck. Luis saw me next and just smiled so warmly. Finally, when I was very close to them, I said "*Hola*," and my sister moved aside so *mi mamá* could see me: she started crying at once. We immediately embraced each other and I cried in *mi mamá's* arms too. I then hugged *mi abuela* and Luis and took a few pictures. I had finally arrived. We were all there together. It was such a great way to start my visit to Colombia. I did not know what we'd be doing in the coming days but I did know that I had to soak everything in that I could because it was one of the biggest events in my life.

Jennifer Beth Capeless was born in Bogotá in June 1987 and was adopted three months later by Michael and Jackie Dovner. At the age of six, her parents enrolled her in karate and within a few years she fell in love with the sport. While attending Simmons College in Boston, she was able to earn her 1st degree black belt in Tae Kwon Do in the summer of 2008. The following spring, she graduated and at the end of 2009 she began working as the logistics manager for her father's coffee company, Boston's Best. During the summer of 2012, she found her biological mother. In November 2014, Jennifer married the love of her life, John Capeless. They live in Massachusetts.

Pushing And Pulling

Jacob Taylor-Mosquera

In that moment I wanted to push her far away from me but I also wanted to pull her closer. It was easily the longest hug of my life and my left sleeve was soaked from the incessant cascade of her tears. I distinctly remember being incapable of forcing myself to cry. This was, after all, the first 10 minutes of meeting my biological mother in Cali, Colombia. If there was ever a moment where I felt tears should jump off of my face, it should have been that moment. The inability to cry was a symptom of how I felt about this woman: happiness for finally meeting her, sadness for her physical situation since she had suffered a lot, and, honestly, I felt resentful. I wanted to hear her reasons why she left me and why I was not worth fighting for. Perhaps the resentment was the dominant emotion.

Twenty years had slipped between us since she had apparently left me in the hospital and kept my birth a secret from her entire family. I use the word "apparently" because she still claims I was stolen by social workers and she had no way to fight the case. It has taken time to accept I will never know the full truth. Thanks to a random television interview, I had already met her extended family months before during my second trip to the country, which lasted nearly eight months in late 2004. To this day there is palpable tension between her and the rest of the family, which I have managed to navigate while living between the U.S. and Europe for work and studies.

That element of pushing away and pulling closer is what I want to discuss in depth and how it has shaped my experience with negotiating adoption. Perhaps the best way to assume this task is by offering the reader a series of confessions and reflections on things I have noticed as unpleasant patterns and which I attribute to adoption. And I should mention I fully recognize my lack of formal training related to the nebulous web of psychology.

Intimate Relationships

In the four serious relationships I have been fortunate enough to have I was the one to terminate them each time, although if we dove into the intricacies of it, you might determine the first was mutual. In any case, I fall hard when the illusions of Love begin to knock at my door. I set things in motion to pull her closer and adhere to the strictest laws of charm I can imagine. This is nothing new; I am certain everyone experiences something similar. The difference is once issues start to arise in the relationship. If I start to detect she is no longer happy with/because of me, I sever the union with a sharpness that leaves us both in a dizzying blur of shock, anger, disappointment, and, ultimately, evaporated trust. This is not a meticulous plan or something I decide with any amount of pleasure. It stings to hurt those you develop a profound adoration for. But it is something I recognize I have done, especially on two occasions, to women I respected immensely. As time passes I reach out to them again, with honest hopes of clinging to their friendship for as long as possible. This effort seems to be 50% successful. On a few occasions I have pushed women away who started to develop stronger feelings for me than I was prepared to have for them. So with relationships I have unconsciously and involuntarily embraced a pull-push-pull pattern, which on a certain level, I readily confess, I am sick of.

Biological Mother

What is arguably the most significant example of my push/pull patterns is the relationship I have with my biological mother, to whom I am unable or possibly unwilling to consign the full title of Mother. That place is already taken. Mother is the one who was there to raise me, to have a meaningful and lasting presence in my life. This is something I feel comfortable with and both of my mothers know: there will be no replacing the one who chose to raise me. I refer to my biological mother by her first name only: Deisy. She refers to me by first name, *hijo* (son) or *corazón* (heart). Twelve years have now passed since we were locked in that hurricane of emotions that was our first embrace, and I still do not trust her completely. The naïveté that clouded my 20-year-old eyes when I first met her has long disappeared. Perhaps it is not fair to dismiss it is mere naïveté. It seems natural that a child would want to trust his or her mother.

When we met I clung to every letter of every word she told me, ultimately falling victim to her relentless verbal assault on the rest of the family to the point where I began turning my back on the people I had spent months building relationships with (extreme pull and push!). It was confusing and frustrating. I heard tales of how an aunt had drowned her first baby in a sink, how cousins had killed people in gangs, and how my grandmother used to beat her and her siblings with machetes and rocks she found on the street.

However, during my trip back to Colombia in 2007, I got to know her a little better. She had either forgotten or completely changed numerous stories about the same family members. The lies kept coming. I gave her money for a bus one day and she returned hours later with a purse full of cigarettes, notably trying to hide them from me, after she had claimed she had never smoked a cigarette in her life.

And then one morning, the distrust came to a boiling point. It was approximately 6:00 a.m. when I awoke to someone unzipping my backpack under the bed. I flipped on the light and saw Deisy standing with her hands behind her back, her eyes fixed on the floor behind her thick glasses. She has been deaf since around my birth, so for us to communicate effectively I write and she reads and responds by speaking in her uniquely squeaky voice, often slurring her speech due to a few jaw surgeries. I scribbled, "Are you alright? Can I help you?" on a piece of paper and showed it to her, to which she replied by throwing my passport on the ground and sobbing quietly. "What do you need my passport for?" I wrote. After she was done crying she said quickly, "I know you need your passport to leave the country so I was going to burn it and that way you can stay and buy me a house." It was a reply that signified the tipping point in my distrust of her. I found it unfathomable that she was prepared to steal from me, never mind the desperate plea for a house, which I can actually comprehend. At the time I felt angry and disappointed and it took approximately two years to realize that I am nobody to judge her, especially if her claims about social workers stealing me are accurate.

If I were in her situation I might have done something similar. In hindsight, I feel as if she has her own pull/push pattern, although I think she truly believes she only pulls. It is clear she does not reflect

78

on how her actions are perceived by others, evidenced in part by the relentless fabricated gossip she spreads about family members in an attempt to keep me to herself when I visit.

The situation with her now is climbing towards more trust...slowly. It is now September and I arrived back in Cali this time in March. We have seen each other two times while living in the same city.

I do not particularly care for who I become when I spend too much time around her (I can feel myself becoming more irritable, less patient, more cautious about what I say and even my body language changes). With the extended family I perceive things to be great. They understand now that I will not be giving them money; I support cousins with their studies and we spend a good amount of time together.

It feels appropriate to admit I harbor ambivalent feelings towards my biological mother, towards adoption in general, and even towards myself. There is a constant internal battle to understand Deisy and share some of the profound adoration, almost idolization, I feel for my adoptive mother. But I have lost that battle time and time again. Maybe I do not even truly want to share. I vacillate between eventually wanting to adopt a child and not, while fully recognizing the decision will not be mine alone.

Conclusion

As for myself, the pull/push factor is still a deep, convoluted issue to be resolved. I am certain it is due to reasons relating to my adoption and I consider it something that could not have been avoided. My adoptive parents raised my sister and me in a fun and loving environment, free of any significant hardship. Of course there were things I wish could have been a part of my childhood like more exposure to Spanish-speaking people or simply living in a more culturally diverse area, but those things were out of my parents' control and there was no Internet in those days. In my opinion, there was nothing they could have done to prevent any of the confusion and frustration I have described here. I mentioned being sick of the pattern regarding intimate relationships but unfortunately I see no magical pill to stop it.

I can only continue to have an inquisitive and thoughtful outlook and aspire to keep learning. Perhaps there really is no need to fix it and I need to simply embrace it as a part of my personality. Only time has the answer.

Jacob Taylor-Mosquera was raised in the Seattle, Washington, area and is currently living in Cali, Colombia, teaching English and translating. In 2017, he plans to return to the U.S. or Europe to pursue a doctoral degree in Latin American studies. Eventually, he would like to be involved in public policy regarding higher education in Colombia. Jacob is single and enjoys playing/coaching soccer, dancing, and traveling.

Swimming Turtle Woman
Gloria Ayshel Amaya

Despite the fact that I had taken a swim to sober up a bit, I still felt my head slightly buzzing as I climbed onto the shore. It was a perfect day. The sun was shining brightly but the thick canopy of trees kept most of the shoreline nicely shaded. The clear river wound its way through the lush mountain landscape. The rains from the previous night had stirred the water, making the river less clear than usual. My family was disappointed. They had wanted to show off the crystal clear water.

It was my second time visiting my first family, my natural family, in Colombia. Each one of them had told me how beautiful the river was, how crystal clear the waters that wove through the mountain-side were, and how we would have so much fun. They told me the *sancocho* we would make at the river would be better than when we had made it the last time *en la calle*, in the street.

I found that hard to believe. I thought back to that first visit with *mi familia*. I was so excited to make *sancocho* with them. *Sancocho* is a traditional stew in Latin America and everyone has his or her own variation. I couldn't wait to have this ancestral dish prepared for me by my mother. We had cooked it in a large pot placed on cinder blocks over a fire in the street. It needs to cook for a long time to soften the meat and tuber vegetables typically used in the stew, which is why we cooked it that way. The fire used less energy/fewer resources than cooking it on a gas stove.

It was everything I had ever dreamed of; me, surrounded by *mi familia*, cooking, laughing, drinking, and then devouring the delicious and nourishing food we had prepared together as a family reunited. Afterward we danced in the street. It was one of the happiest nights of my life.

How could this be better, I thought? They assured me it would be.

Armed with plenty of *aguardiente* (the national alcoholic beverage of Colombia,) an enormous pot, and the food that the women in my

81

family had prepped, we set to take off for the river. Most of the family clambered into the back of a *camioneta* (an open-back truck) while the rest of us took off on motorcycles. There were 15 adults and 4 kids; we were quite the crew.

When we arrived at the river, the women immediately set to work. My grandmother, the matriarch, and my mother gathered sticks and started the fire for cooking. As the fire started smoking, the *aguardiente* started flowing. Shot after shot after shot. *Guaro*, as we Colombians call it, has a relatively low alcohol content, and even though it roughly translates as firewater, it goes down surprisingly smooth—making it quite easy to drink. I couldn't tell you how many shots I had but it was enough for me to decide a submerging in the cool river might help me clear my head a bit so I could keep up with my family for the rest of the day. Colombians love to party. So I dove in. I swam through the refreshing waters.
I didn't open my eyes but somehow I could see the sunbeams illuminating the rocks below me and the translucent water ahead. I saw the life I would have had coinciding with the life I lived. Two lives intersected in a moment in time that I never thought possible.

The boisterousness of my family's feast was diluted by the sound of the rushing river as I swam beneath the surface. It drowned out all thoughts I had about why this was the life chosen for me. For a moment, I just was.

Baptized in the mountain waters of my motherland I felt at peace.

It was sublime. I usually feel at home when I am in Colombia, when I am with my first family. Even though I grew up in the States, I don't feel like an outsider with them; somehow, they make me feel like I've just been away awhile. Like a kid who's been away at boarding school and is home for the summer.

Somewhat cleansed of my drunkenness, I came up for air, my face turned toward the sun. I felt restored and so I walked out and onto the shore feeling more clearheaded and at peace, not wanting to forget one moment of this precious reunion.

As I stepped out of the water, several family members shouted at me, "Did you see the turtle?!"

I was stunned. "What?" I asked, incredulous. "There was a turtle swimming with you. Didn't you see the turtle?" Now they were in disbelief that I hadn't seen it. Suddenly my brain was foggy again and my cleansing river swim was forgotten. I shook my head to clear my eyes of tears and my mind of the unbelievable, but it was too late, the tears came anyway.

***

Several weeks before this trip I had sought counsel. Even though it was my second time being with my family, it was still only my second time being with my family. I was nervous. The first time I met them, a family friend, who is Colombian, and who acted not only as my translator but my emotional support as well, had joined me. This time, I was acting as the support and translator for my biological aunt who I was bringing to meet the family for the first time, but that is another story for another time. The point is, I didn't feel ready to take on such a role even though I had agreed to it. Of course, sleepless nights and panic attacks ensued but being the ever-diligent self-healer that I am, I sought help.

I had a co-worker who was a woman who did intuitive Reiki sessions. I, myself, had taken the first level of Reiki training from her and had had such a profound experience in her class that I decided to go to her for guidance, healing, and grounding prior to my trip.

I sat in the dimly lit room facing this woman to whom I had turned for guidance. Her flaxen curls surrounded her head like a halo, her eyes were closed, and her deep reassuring voice told me of the ancestors that had come to great me for our healing session. She declared a female elder had stepped forward to speak on behalf of the group. An elder, who had the energy of a turtle: slow, wise, and deliberate. She marveled at the fact that this elder showed up like that and explained that this turtle-like energy was very unique and quite different from most spirit guides. She was especially moved because that morning she had returned to her home to retrieve a certain talisman that she knew she would need for our session. It was a turtle rattle made by a shaman.

This spirit guide spoke through my Reiki master to me. She gave me messages about my upcoming trip to my homeland. This magic, turtle-like ancestor helped calm my fears about my second reunion with a family I still wanted to learn so much about. I felt reassured that I was doing the right thing, that I would indeed be able to help my aunt and be a good source of support for her. Part of being an adoptee, for me, has always been doubting myself. It has also been about seeking validation that I am actually here for a reason. This intuitive session calmed my fears and I felt reassured that I was, in fact, doing the right thing by going home and reuniting a family torn apart by dire circumstances.

When we started the Reiki-healing portion of the session, she took out the turtle rattle and shook it all around me. The rhythmic dancing of the seeds inside the shell created a sort of music that put me in a trance and carried me off to another world in which I was free of anxiety and self-doubt. My energy and mind were cleared and I was able to focus on the natural flow within my body. I finally felt grounded enough to embark on my next journey home.

Weeks after that session, I arrived in Colombia for this second reunion. I rode through the mountains on my brother's motorcycle to my hometown. I had held tightly to him, grateful to be there and not on the crowded bus with the rest of the family. The air was cool and sent chills up my bare arms. The hum of the *moto* put me into the same type of trance that cleared my mind and soul that the turtle rattle had, and I was thankful for the space. I was able to see, smell, and take in everything around me. The mountains we rode through dripped an emerald landscape shimmering with the possibility of a life that was whole and complete and un-needing of any validation for purpose. There were immense, cotton candy clouds above that parted to reveal a burst of sun shining down from the heavens and I felt an overwhelming sense that my ancestors were welcoming me home. My heart burst open and tears flowed from my eyes and down my face. The gratitude I had in that moment was overwhelming. I was finally going home. On my previous trip, I hadn't taken the two-and-a-half-hour journey to my birthplace. Now I was, and I held tight to my brother as my ancestors whispered a welcoming to me through the trees that needed no translation.

That leads us back to the river where this story started.

A swim with a turtle. In the river of my birthplace.

Was it a sign from the heavens? Was it reassurance that I was, in fact, in exactly the right place, as every spiritual guru would like you to believe?

It was all a little too much for me to hold in so it spilled out of my eyes in the form of tears.

So there I was, trying to hold it together but failing. And my family not understanding why I was crying about swimming with a turtle and I can't explain anything to them because I don't speak the same language and suddenly I don't feel like I belong anymore

I am an outsider.

No longer the boarding school daughter returned home but the daughter who was never supposed to happen at all. The daughter born at an inopportune time.

A daughter relinquished.

A daughter who ended up in a land so far away from where she belonged that she had spent a lifetime trying to make her way back. And though she was home physically, it still wasn't home really.

She no longer spoke the same language as her kin and here she was crying on the shores of a river in her native land but unable to express the significance of any of it. English may as well be her native tongue now, but it is a language she was forced to learn and in doing so she lost her voice for there is so much sorrow wrapped up in her mother tongue that neither Spanish nor English feels right rolling out of her mouth now. Her tongue bound by the trauma of losing her *mami* when she was two years old.

So I remain silent. And I weep. And my family tries to conjecture what I am feeling. "She misses her family," they suppose. And I do. But not in the way they imagine. They think I am missing my two daughters and husband I left in the States for this reunion trip, but really it is them that I am missing. *Mi familia.* The one that is standing right in front of me, the ones I belong to but don't know. The family who was separated from me by a continent, an ocean, a lost language, and lost culture. The family that belongs to me but that I can't communicate with, at least verbally. And for someone to whom communication is of the utmost importance this is a huge blow. However, there are other ways of communication. I looked around me and saw concern in the eyes of my siblings. In their eyes I could see the love that bound us, so even though I couldn't fully articulate what was happening in that moment I knew that, despite the great divide between our lives and all that we had lost, we had not lost love. In fact, the love that remained was as vast as the mountains we were standing in and as deep as the ocean that had separated us.   They say blood is thicker than water. And here I had found my blood, *mi sangre, mi familia,* in the water of a river in the mountains where I was born. An ancestor, swimming beside me in the shape of a turtle. An ancestor as a symbol to show me where I came from, and where I am, and to confirm that I am exactly in the right place.

Ancient mythology credits the turtle as a symbol of uniting heaven and earth, with the shell representing heaven and the square underside a symbol of the earth. The gift of seeing a turtle represents the wisdom of knowing that all things come in perfect and divine timing. In life there is no destination but a series of journeys and we ride the wave, surrender to the tide, and trust we will end up in the right place.

And so I have. After a lifetime of feeling displaced, I found my way home
I don't know why I have been granted this privilege of reconnecting with my first family but I have been. This is my path, my journey for this lifetime and I accept that.   So, finally I looked at *mi familia,* standing in front of me with their uncertain faces, the sun shining down on them from the heavens and I said, "Yes, I miss my family."

They simply hugged me, laughed, and poured me another shot of *guaro*.

In the days that followed, my turtle-like ancestor guide kept following me. One day, I went to my grandmother's house and the first thing she did was bring out her pet turtle to show me. I was dumbfounded. I mean, seriously? My grandmother has a pet turtle? I was muted, again lacking the language to discuss the synchronicity of it all. After that, I ended up telling my aunt, who I was traveling with, the whole story. I told her about the Reiki healer, and my turtle-like ancestor that had spoken through her. I needed someone to understand that what had happened at the river was bigger than I could explain.

Some days after that, we were having dinner with some extended family that we were staying with. Suddenly, our host jumped up because she wanted to show us something. What she brought to the table looked like a dinosaur egg. I held it and she told me to open it so I did. Inside was a fossilized baby turtle. My aunt and I exchanged glances and laughed.

The following day as we were exploring the city of Medellin, my aunt started yelling, "Look, look! Hurry! We need to take a photo!" I looked across the highway and there was a huge mural of a turtle. I quickly turned to face her with the turtle mural behind me as she snapped my picture. The family thought we were crazy to get so excited about some graffiti that was everywhere in the city but we just laughed and exclaimed to one another how crazy it was that these turtles were following me everywhere.

The signs are there if you bother to pay attention.

One night my brother asked about the turtle. I searched my brain for the right words. It is so frustrating trying to communicate meaningful things when your Spanish language skills are so limited. I was completely unable to find any words to tell him about the guide, so instead I tried to focus on the meaning of the turtle. He understood the symbolism of what a turtle represents. At least, I like to believe he did. That's still the problem with where I'm at in relearning my first language. I think I understand what's being said—and what I'm saying—but there is a chance I could be completely wrong. I hope one day to be totally fluent and at ease speaking Spanish. I hope one day I know not only the basic words for communicating with *mi familia* but the poetic words as well. Spanish is such a beautiful and expressive language and not only do I long to reclaim that missing part of myself but I long to have a fluid conversation with my family. One in which I have complete certainty that we understand one another. I hope one day to be able to tell them the story of our turtle-like ancestor that calmed my fears and swam with me in the clear mountain waters of our homeland.

On the other hand, I was so glad I had shared my story with my aunt. It had made the whole thing less heavy. That is the power of sharing your story. Once you release it from the confines of your mind it has less power over your thoughts. You can see it outside of yourself, thus you can see yourself from the outside as well and the healing can begin.

I was also able to communicate with my Reiki guide, whom I had been anxious to tell about my journey with the turtles. I wrote to her and sent some pictures as well. She responded very quickly and simply said, "That's beautiful! I'm happy for you. Your new name is 'Swimming Turtle Woman.'"

Gloria Ayshel Amaya was born in San Rafael, Antioquia, in 1977. She lived with her natural mother for two years before she was entered into the adoption system. She was adopted in 1980 and moved to Stillwater, Minnesota, where she was raised. She has reunited with her natural family, thanks to Facebook, and is in constant communication with them.

Gloria currently resides in Minneapolis, Minnesota. She loves to travel and would love to move back to Colombia so she could be closer to her family and live in the land of eternal spring.

Coming Full Circle

Elissa Victoria Doell (Victoria Martinez)

Since I was a little girl of about eight or nine years old, I have always felt a little different. As an adoptee, it was harder for me to fit in with the other kids. My classmates thought it was weird that I was adopted. They would say my birthmother must not have loved or wanted me, and they began to tease me. It was at that time when I started to ask myself those same questions—*Did my birthmother love me? Did she want me?*—and I would think of her often. My (adoptive) mother, Barbara, has always shared as much information with me as possible regarding my adoption. For as long as I can remember, I thought about trying to find my birthmother. I wanted to learn more about my Colombian culture and family, but most importantly I wanted to know why she put me up for adoption. However, I was very afraid of getting a negative response. *What if she doesn't want to talk to me? Will she reject me reaching out to her? Will she deny my existence?* are questions I asked myself. My husband, Keith, and I had countless conversations about the pros and cons of trying to find her. I still wasn't completely sure if this was the best decision for me emotionally, but I was comforted knowing that I had an amazing amount of love and support from my family. I finally decided to embark on the journey to search for my birthmother, Blanca Marisol.

I met Carolina through one of my online Colombian adoptee support groups. After a few conversations with her I knew she would be the perfect investigator to help me. I sent her all of my paperwork on August 13, 2013, and only one day later I got the message, "I found her." I immediately started crying. I thought to myself, *Could this possibly be true?* This was such an unknown part of my life that I had created endless scenarios about, and I was finally about to get some answers. My heart felt like it was beating out of my chest. Carolina was on the phone with my mother and she relayed to me that I have two sisters that live in Miami, Florida, and a little brother who still lives in Colombia with my mom. Coincidentally, I grew up 20 minutes from Miami but currently reside in Maryland. When Carolina gave me the links to their Facebook pages my husband and I were astounded at the resemblance. I called my mom (adoptive mother) to share the exciting news with her. She was speechless. Before she told my father, she simply showed him a picture of my older sister, Andrea. He said, "Oh, that's a nice picture of Elissa." My mom replied, "That's actually Elissa's birth sister. She found them!"

The next month I spent countless hours on the phone with my newfound sisters, Deysy and Andrea, and within just a few short weeks, I was on a plane to Ft. Lauderdale, Florida, to meet them. At the time, my birth uncle and grandmother also lived with them. On September 9, 2013, I got to meet four members of my birth family. They embraced me like they had known me forever. As grateful and happy as I was to meet them, something was still missing.

In the summer of 2015 I got the news that Blanca and my little brother, Cristian, were finally moving to Florida. In April of 2016 we flew down to Florida to meet them. The plan was to meet them at my sister Andrea's house. I didn't start getting nervous until the GPS said we were five minutes away. I literally felt like I was going to throw up. I was so unbelievably nervous and I couldn't stop shaking. When we arrived, I got out of the car and hugged my brother-in-law, Tuscany, who was waiting for us outside. I walked in the house and hugged my gorgeous sister Andrea and then, finally, I experienced the long awaited, 25-year overdue embrace with my beautiful mother. We held each other so tight and just cried for what felt like forever. Then from behind the corner I saw my sweet 20-year-old brother with the most genuine tears streaming down his face. Again, just one of the most amazing and unforgettable embraces I've ever experienced. After that we talked for about an hour; we shared life experiences and asked questions that we had for one another. Then my (adoptive) family pulled up to Andrea's house. Immediately after walking in the door, my two mothers shared a warm hug and told each other "Thank you." At that moment, I felt complete. Now, I feel as though my adoption story has come full circle. Never in my wildest dreams could I have pictured both of my mothers hugging each other. It was truly a special moment.

Currently, I still keep in touch with my birth family. My sister Deysy has even visited us in Maryland with her husband and their beautiful little daughter. I Skype with all of my birth family every now and then and message them through social media a few times a week.

Even with the language barrier between us, we are able to have conversations by using our translation applications. Unfortunately, my birth grandmother, Mitalu, just passed away in August of 2016. I feel very blessed to have met her and my other family members. It's a dream come true to know them and be forming this lifelong relationship with all of them.

This has been a very emotional experience for me and certainly not the easiest. However, the most difficult part of this process has been dealing with the emotions of everyone else. I don't want either family to feel loved any less. Both my adoptive family and birth family are very important to me. At the end of the day the most important thing to remember, as an adoptee, is this is MY journey and even though it can be emotionally hard at times, it is worth the lifelong relationships.

Elissa Victoria Doell (Victoria Martinez) was adopted from FANA in Bogotá, Colombia, at four months old. She was brought to Staten Island, New York, where she lived until the age of three. She grew up in South Florida where she went to school and enjoyed performing in musical theater for 14 years. She moved to Maryland in 2010 where she currently resides with her husband and two beautiful sons. She is the founder and operator of The Early Explorers, a Family Child Care facility in Harford County, MD. She is excited about expanding to a commercial childcare center in summer 2017. Her interests include singing, dancing, traveling, and spending time with her family. She is honored to be apart of such a special piece and to share a bond with the other writers of this book.

Appendix
Q&A With The Authors

What advice would you give to other adoptees, regardless of where they are on their adoption journey?

- Own your story. Embrace it. Wrap yourself in it like a swaddled baby. Above all though, talk about it. Hopefully with your adoptive family! Certainly with ones you trust and/or love.

- It is OK to change your mind about an issue at any point, especially as you learn more and hear of other experiences. At some point you may feel happy or satisfied with your adoption, at another point you may feel it was detrimental and a breaking point in your life that you wish had never happened. But reach out and connect, online, through DNA, via investigators, and in person and other ways, with other adoptees.

- Life is short, and my adoption was out of my control and is nothing I should be ashamed of. It wasn't until I realized this that I could truly begin to feel comfortable in my own skin for the first time.

- Above all, seek the help and moral support of other adoptees. They are the only ones who can truly empathize with your situation, feelings, and the processes that you need to go through.

Based on your experience, what would you recommend to adoptees who are struggling with their identity and/or adoption-related thoughts and feelings?

- I strongly recommend working through your adoption with professional help/psychiatrist. It is worth it. Nobody should go through this without professional help. It is just too hard and too painful. Actually, it is even risky doing it without such help.

- In my experience it throws you off balance completely/messes with everything you know and feel. Without guidance, one can easily get lost.

- The advice I would give others with the similar past would be to never give up hope and to forgive. Forgiveness not only sets the abusers free (for those adoptees who were abused) but sets you free as well. I'm still learning that forgiveness and letting go are a process; and I'm still learning this process every day.

- Adoptees of color in white families have the unique advantage of seeing both the black and white sides of things in society, for lack of a better expression. Use your story to better empathize with others.

- Adoption has made adoptees 'bi-family,' with both a birth and adoptive family who both shape who we are in ways we often are unaware of ourselves. Professional counseling by an adoption-savvy therapist is very helpful to any of us during the course of our lives, particularly the difficult times.

What advice would you give to adoptees who are considering searching or are in the process of searching for their mother/family of origin?

- If you decide to begin a search, do your best to not create a perfect fantasy situation. Ideally, this will prevent you from suffering profound disappointment. It may sound cruel, but I wish someone would have told me to expect the worst when I started my search.

- Before starting to search, prepare, prepare, prepare! Join a local support group for adoptees in your community. If one doesn't exist, consider starting one. Listening and talking to other adoptees is invaluable. Read adoption literature that addresses the trauma that can occur due to mother-child separation. Begin therapy with an adoption-savvy therapist. Join online groups for adoptees. Join online adoption groups for adoptees and mothers of adoption loss.

- In order to truly understand your thoughts and feelings, I think it is essential to also understand those of our "other half": our natural mothers.

- If you decide not to search for your biological family, please find some way to let your birthmom know you are ok. She will never forget about you and she will never know if you are safe and healthy if you don't let her know.

- If you decide to search for your family, please know you may encounter something that may not be pleasing to hear.

- My mistake was that I didn't seek help in the searching process and unification process, but only afterwards. I would do this differently if I could do it again. I recommend following your heart and truly listening to what your inner voice tells you to do. Be honest with yourself and with your biological family. Work through things together—it is as difficult for them, as it is for you. You have to learn to be a family again; it will take time.

What concrete steps have you taken/can an adoptee take to make peace with their adoption?

- The truth encompasses everything—it is holistic—from family relations of all kinds (blood, adopted), to friends, to culture, to territory, to home, to space..., to the food we eat every day. I cope by living and embodying a hybrid lifestyle of a postmodern Euro-Colombian woman. I connect to my Colombian roots on a daily basis, e.g., by speaking Spanish every day, as well as consolidating my European upbringing and postmodern education. I acknowledge that I am both yet neither and have no country that represents my composition. I live in the "Third Space;" it is my home.

- Use your story to do something meaningful. Whether it's putting together a book like this, standing up for the underprivileged, or simply loving someone deeply and unconditionally.

What would you like to say to natural/first/birth/biological mothers?

- Please understand that your son or daughter have had a life without you for many years.

- Depending on their experiences as a child, their connections with their adoptive parents and other life factors, they may or may not establish a close relationship with you. Please do not ask them for money because this could ultimately push them away from you.

- Reunion is not easy. It takes time to get to know each other after years of being separated. Be patient, honest, and kind with yourself and with your adult child. Seeking professional help to deal with all of the emotions is nothing to be ashamed about; in fact, it can be very helpful.

If you could speak directly to adoptive parents, what would you say?

- Please be understanding and supportive if your child wants to find their birth family someday. Please don't see it as a threat but as a time where you can become closer with your child.

- Respect and honor where your child is from. With technology and the abundance of available knowledge, there are no excuses to not teach your child about where s/he is from and to make their original culture part of your multicultural family.

- The biggest piece of advice I can provide to adoptive parents is to make sure your kids are constantly exposed to their birth culture and language. Try to demonstrate empathy as they navigate through their adoption experience good or bad or both, and most importantly remember it is not about you. Honor and respect the feelings of your child and any desire to search for their roots. Read up on early childhood trauma and separation anxiety. And I cannot recommend more following all of the principles of attachment parenting.

- Any member of the adoption triad may change their views on search and reunion at any time. Just because a birth parent decided to make an adoption plan 20 years ago, doesn't mean they don't want to know about their son or daughter, or meet them now.